The Art of Positive Thinking

Eliminate Negative Thinking I Emotional Intelligence I Stop Overthinking: A Self Help Book to Developing Mindfulness and Overcoming Negative Thoughts

ELIZABETH R. BROWN

ISBN - 9798862579062

Contetns

Introduction 5

Chapter 1. Benefits of Positive Thinking 7
- *Positive Thinking – It's Not Just Being Happy* 8
- *Benefits to Help Keep You Motivated to Think Positive* 10

Chapter 2. Learning about Mindfulness 15
- *Understanding What Mindfulness Is* 16
- *Learning How to Be Mindful* 21
- *Other Ways to Practice Being Mindful* 23

Chapter 3. Understanding and Developing Emotional Intelligence 29
- *The Four Attributes of Emotional Intelligence* 30
- *How Emotional Intelligence Affects You* 31
- *Developing Emotional Intelligence* 35

Chapter 4. Understanding Your Own Mindset 41
- *The Repetitive Nature of Thinking* 42
- *Split Thoughts up According to Helpful and Limiting* 44

Chapter 5. Easy Actions to Increase Positive Thinking 47
- *Your Daily Affirmations* 48
- *Make Time to Meditate* 53
- *Think of Three Positives* 56
- *Best Case Scenario* 62
- *Practice Positive Lessons from Failure* 66
- *Take a Mental Break* 70

Chapter 6. Spreading the Positivity 73
- *Smile a Bit more* 74
- *Help When You Can* 78
- *Be Less Negative When Speaking or Acting* 82
- *Spread Positivity on Social Media* 85
- *Be Free with Compliments* 89

Chapter 7. Practicing Gratitude to Improve Positive Thinking 95
- *Be Observant* 96
- *Start or End Your Day by Being Thankful for Three Things* 98
- *It Can Always Be Worse ...* 99

• *Journal about Your Experiences* 101
• *Get Creative* 103

Chapter 8. Becoming More Aware of Negative Thinking 107
• *Practice Mindfulness More Often* 108
• *Realize When Your Thoughts are Distorted* 111
• *Be More Compassionate with Yourself* 114
• *Spend Time Noticing the Positives* 116

Chapter 9. The Role of Relationships in Positive Thinking 119
• *Building and Sustaining Positive Family Dynamics* 120
• *Friends and Positivity* 122
• *Romantic Relationships* 125
• *Dealing with Workplace Relationships* 128
• *Healing from Past Relationships* 130

Chapter 10. Maintaining Positive Thinking in Chaos and Rougher Times 133
• *Give Yourself Permission to Think without Trying to Change It* 134
• *Accept Help* 135
• *Practice Your Favorite Positive Thought Activities* 138
• *Exercise Mindfulness and Your Body* 139
• *Seek out Positivity* 143

Chapter 11. Tips and Tricks to Keep You Going 145
• *Get out in nature* 146
• *Indulge in a Small Guilty Pleasure* 150
• *Try Something New* 153
• *Indulge in Music* 155
• *Pay Attention to What You Are Consuming in the Digital World* 157

Chapter 12. Conclusion: The Everlasting Journey of Positive Thought 163
• *Crafting a Positive Vision for Tomorrow* 163
• *Committing to a Lifetime of Continued Positivity* 164

Appendix 167
• *Glossary* 167
• *Recommended Reading* 169
• *Bibliography* 170

Disclaimer 179

Introduction

Some people are born optimistic, so positive thinking comes naturally to them. Others live in environments and locations that make it easier to adopt an optimistic outlook. According to Our World in Data, people tend to be more optimistic about their own futures, indicating an innate bias on an individual level, meaning people are more likely to be naturally optimistic. Overall, a person is more likely to be optimistic than realistic when it comes to their own future, which is probably for the best when one considers that newlyweds are more likely to entirely reject the idea that they will get divorced. However, people tend to lose that optimization the larger the scale they are asked to consider.

While people tend to be optimistic overall, it is easy to get bogged down in negative thinking and to undermine oneself. More importantly, researchers have found links between the way a person thinks and both their physical and mental health. Numerous studies have shown that positive thinking tends to help people live longer and be healthier. According to John Hopkins, if a person has a family history of heart disease, being more positive reduces the risk of heart attack by a third. There are many reasons why positive thinking can help a person be more physically healthy, including the fact that people are more likely to exercise when they are feeling well, which means they will feel better, creating a cycle of positivity that can help a person be healthier.

Fortunately, you don't have to be an optimist to be able to think positively. At some point in your life, you are all but guaranteed to feel some depression and anxiety (usually not at the same time – think about the anxiety you feel before a test or job interview compared to the depression you feel when a pet dies, or you go through a breakup). Even optimists feel these negative emotions – they are a part of being human. It's ok to feel anxious or depressed, but when these conditions are caused by outside sources, you can work to think positively to help yourself work through them.

This book is not meant to replace medical advice. If you suffer from depression, anxiety, and other mental health issues or if you experience regular negative thoughts that align more with one of these problems, it is best to seek help from a professional.

By the time you have read to the end of this book, you should have a better understanding of how you can start altering the way you think to improve your life. It doesn't mean ignoring your problems or being obnoxiously positive – it means actively working to keep your thoughts from spiraling down. This will definitely be a journey, and you can't expect to start thinking positively right off the bat. It will take practice and work because what you are doing is creating a new habit in the way you think. Though it is going to take effort and time, ultimately it is well worth it for all of the positive effects you get from taking a more positive approach to life. Once you get accustomed to thinking positively, it will be a lot easier to maintain that attitude.

CHAPTER 1

Benefits of Positive Thinking

It's fine for researchers to say that there are a lot of benefits to thinking positively, but it can definitely feel like they are asking for the impossible. When you are bogged down with bills, chores, and other things you don't want to do, it can feel like being told to be positive is just one more demand on your time.

Fortunately, thinking positively isn't the same as being positive. We all know someone who seems excessively positive, and that is not only exhausting but a bit annoying. That's not what researchers mean when they say thinking positively has a lot of health benefits. It is literally in your head, so there doesn't need to be any physical signs that you are thinking positive – that's probably going to happen just as a part of the shift in your thinking, but it's not where you need to place your focus.

This chapter will help you understand what kind of positive thinking is beneficial to your health and what those benefits are. Knowing what the benefits are will also help serve as a motivator when things feel a little too out of control or it is rough to keep trying to think positively.

Positive Thinking - It's Not Just Being Happy

One of the misconceptions about positive thinking is that it is always about yourself and whatever you are doing. But being able to think positively goes well beyond being able to put a positive spin on one of your own problems. It's about being able to start changing your attitude so that you can have more positive responses to things going on around you.

For example, learning that your friend has gotten a promotion at work is news that should make you happy. Sure, there may be a bit of jealousy or other aspects that leave you feeling a little unhappy, but you love your friend. The fact that your friend got a promotion is positive, and you should focus on the positives, especially since this will likely help your friend's current situation. Instead of focusing on the fact that you didn't get a promotion, think about the positives that are likely to happen to your friend as a result of the promotion. This could be a bit harder if the promotion means they have to move away from you, but odds are it will benefit their life. And your friend's success is something that you should be happy to celebrate.

Maybe you put together a detailed plan for your birthday party, but everything goes sideways right from the beginning. Instead of getting upset and angry, figure out how to turn the unexpected into a good time. After all, things don't have to go as planned for everyone to have fun. It's your birthday! Have fun and keep thinking of things that you can do to enjoy what you have, instead of focusing on how your plan quickly fell apart.

Perhaps one of the biggest things that people miss when it comes to thinking positively is gratitude. We tend to focus so much on the things we want that we fail to really appreciate what we have. Sure, there is always someone who is more successful, more capable, more intelligent, or more skilled, but there are also plenty of people who are less successful, less capable, less intelligent, or less skilled than you. Instead of measuring yourself against others though, focus on what you have and learn to be thankful for it. Some of the most impressive stories are those about people in horrible situations who still manage to find things to be grateful for in their lives. Stop making life about what you don't have and pay attention to what you do have.

There are many facets of positive thinking, and they all revolve around the idea of actively resisting negative thoughts. If you've ever sat with a group of people and listened to them complain incessantly, you know exactly how you feel when exposed to a lot of negative thinking. You aren't likely to want to talk to those people again because you probably did not enjoy your time with them.

Thinking positively isn't something that you are going to be able to do overnight, especially if you are more pessimistic by nature. Most people aren't in the habit of injecting regular positive thoughts into their day, meaning there are a lot of unhealthy thinking habits that need to be counteracted. You probably didn't become a negative thinker in a matter of days, so you shouldn't expect to be able to turn your thought patterns around in under a week. It will be work, but ultimately it will be one of the best things you can do for yourself.

Positive thinking, which we could also call emotional intelligence, is not necessarily something that one is born with, but it can absolutely be developed and nurtured. This capacity to identify, express, and manage our feelings, to empathize and understand the feelings of other people, and to use these understandings to guide our thoughts and actions, is vital to fostering a positive outlook.

Comprehending and managing our own emotions is the first step. Picture emotional intelligence as a house where the foundation comprises self-awareness and self-regulation. Self-awareness includes the ability to recognize our own emotions and how they affect thoughts and actions. It's about understanding personal strengths and limitations and developing a strong sense of self-confidence. Developing self-awareness can begin with simple exercises. Start each day by identifying your emotional state. Are you feeling frustrated, calm, exhausted, or excited? Self-awareness also means understanding how your emotions might affect others. Pushing negativity onto others might shift the burden, but it can damage relationships. Instead, work on recognizing when you're on the verge of unproductive negativity.

Next, we use self-awareness to master self-regulation – resisting disruptive impulses, maintaining standards of honesty and integrity, and applying flexibility to handle change. Self-regulation comes to the fore in affirming our ability to control or divert our disruptive emotions and the propensity to adapt to changing circumstances. This is not about suppressing emotions, but rather adequately processing feelings. Let's say a flashing red light signals danger and naturally generates anxiety. Acknowledging the alarm, understanding its significance, and using it to navigate a path to safety encapsulates the essence of emotional intelligence.

When applied correctly, these tools of emotional intelligence give birth to a sense of optimism and positivity. You'll understand emotional triggers, and instead of letting them dictate your mood, you can manage or even reframe them. For instance, starting a daunting new project might induce anxiety. Still, by understanding this feeling as a natural reaction to uncertainty, you can manage it, even reframing it as excitement about the learning opportunity this project brings.

Benefits to Help Keep You Motivated to Think Positive

Since you are in for a good bit of work to change the way you think, it will be helpful to know exactly how much you stand to gain by continuing your efforts to think positively. That way, when you are feeling like it is too much work, you can refer to the benefits to keep yourself motivated. Over time, you may even start to notice some of these benefits in your personal life – and people around you will probably start to notice the changes too.

Probably the benefit that connects with most people is that positive thinking can increase a person's life span. It seems more like something out of science fiction, but studies have repeatedly shown that people who have a more positive outlook tend to live longer than people who don't. Even among people diagnosed with the same fatal illness, such as cancer, the people who are more positive will likely live longer. Researchers have a lot of theories on the reason for this fact, but it is harder to specify exactly what it is that helps extend the lifespan of positive thinkers. They don't have to understand the reasons to see the results though. With so many studies over decades worth of data and research showing a positive correlation between positive thinking and longer life, it is obvious that there is something about this mindset that is incredibly beneficial to longevity.

Unsurprisingly, being able to think positively also helps you to better cope with stress and to be more proactive when a situation is more stressful. Instead of being overwhelmed, you are far more likely to act to help mitigate the problem and relieve some of the stress. For example, if you are stressed at work, thinking positively can help you remember to take a step back, remove yourself from the environment for a bit (even if that means going outside for a quick walking break), and then try to find a solution to the problem. A positive mindset is incredibly powerful when it comes to combating stress because it tends to make people much more proactive. When you aren't simply dismissing possible solutions because you don't see the value or don't *think* they will work, you are much more likely to find a solution faster.

Positive thinking can help to lower the risk of depression. This doesn't mean that you won't feel depressed, just that you are less likely to get depressed as easily as those who think negatively. This is because when you think positive, you are less inclined to simply give up and think there's nothing you can do. This does not mean that you should try to "think positive" to get out of a depression because it is not a cure for depression. Those who naturally suffer from depression typically have a biological imbalance that causes the problem, and they should talk to a professional to help with the problem. Similarly, if you lose your job, have to move, or someone dies, you cannot think your way out of the depression you are almost guaranteed to feel in these situations. Positive thinking can help, but you should talk to a professional. What positive thinking does is to help you prevent other depressive episodes tied to factors like seasons, stagnation, or just feeling blah. This is because you are able to see the good, as well as the bad, keeping you from the downward mental spiral that leads to depression.

People who think positively are also at a lower risk of cardiovascular disease. This is another benefit that researchers know is tied to positive thinking, but they are still working to understand why. The answer is probably tied to a number of reasons, such as being more proactive, being more likely to exercise, and worrying a lot less. The odds are that there are a lot of contributing factors to why positive thinking helps your cardiovascular system, but it definitely makes it worthwhile to keep working on positive thinking to gain this benefit.

One benefit that you may not expect is that if you think positively, you have a better tolerance for pain. This benefit definitely requires more research to understand the connection, but medical professionals have long known that their patients who have a more positive outlook on their situation are better able to deal with the pain they feel.

Another surprising benefit is that you will have better resistance to diseases like the common cold and the flu. So far, it is thought that this is because positive thinking is tied to a better immune system, making your system better able to combat common ailments. Again, medical professionals are still working to understand *why* this is the case, but they are no longer uncertain that there is a direct correlation. If you want one more way of fighting off something that is all but certain, you can do a bit more positive thinking while you are drinking your orange juice to boost your immune system.

If you are having trouble finding motivation to fight through some particularly negative thoughts, just consider how much healthier you can be by successfully injecting some positive thoughts into that negativity. Over time, you may notice that you haven't had a cold in years, that your lower back doesn't hurt as much as it used to, or that you just generally feel better. The benefits are not just about being in a better mental state, but about being healthier overall. That's the best benefit that positive thinking has to offer.

CHAPTER 2

Learning about Mindfulness

Mindfulness sounds like a buzzword, but it is actually a word that people use far more often than they realize. Usually, parents will use the word when talking with their kids, saying things like "Be mindful as you cross the street," or "Just be mindful as you cut the vegetables." Mindfulness is really just an extension of this; it simply means being aware and attentive of what you are doing and of the things that are happening around you. We all know that we should be more mindful of ourselves and our surroundings, but it isn't nearly as easy these days because there is always so much going on. If you've ever gotten home after a long day at work and find that you can't remember the full drive – let alone your full day – it's because you have become accustomed to going on autopilot and just carrying on with your normal routine.

Learning how to be mindful is important to changing your thought process, but before you can do that, you have to become aware of the way you think. The more you practice mindfulness, the more you will understand your current thought process. This is essential before you can really start changing it. Everyone starts from a different point, and that may change the length of time you spend in the different phases of the process. For example, if you find that you already tend to think positively, you will just need to encourage these thoughts, especially when things get a little rougher. If you find you tend toward thinking more negative thoughts, you are going to have more work to do in the beginning to reprogram your thought process.

This chapter provides the tools you need to start adjusting your thought process and lets you know how to use those tools.

Understanding What Mindfulness Is

Being fully present is something that children do incredibly well and adults don't. The older we get, the more we tend to think about the future, losing focus on what is happening around us at this moment. Untethering our thoughts from the present means missing out on a lot of the world around us.

It's understandable that you are prone to do this as an adult. As children, there is always so much to learn that being present is easy. School offers a lot of new information, even when it isn't a subject that particularly interests you. When they get out of school, kids have homework, chores, and a lot of time to play. They may play video games or watch TV, which pulls them out of reality, but even then, they tend to return to the present more quickly once they are done.

Adults have a far less varied life, making it more likely they will spend more time not focusing on the world around them. Autopilot becomes a large part of the day, meaning adults are far less active in the way they think, allowing negative thought patterns to take an increasingly larger part of the thought process. It also means that a lot of us are far less aware of our thought process because of how disconnected we are.

Before you can do anything else, you have to learn how to be mindful again. What sounds like an easy task will almost certainly prove to be a more difficult task than you expect, and the older you are, the more difficult this will probably prove to be. After all, if you have a couple of decades of practice putting your mind on autopilot, it's going to take a lot more effort to pay attention to your thoughts and surroundings.

It is definitely worth the effort though as you'll be able to enjoy the world around you a bit more since you will be more present. Even teenagers tend to be less mindful, though the problem is more likely to stem from emotions and all of the physical changes than from habit.

Being mindful isn't about subjugating your mind and focusing solely on one thing. Being mindful just means being more aware of the world around you.

Embracing mindfulness as opposed to living life on autopilot is an essential transformative shift that can greatly enhance your emotional intelligence and help keep negativity at bay. Let's delve deeper into how this change can manifest rewarding benefits. To begin with, embodying mindfulness means fostering an active, deliberate awareness of your present experience. It's about fully immersing yourself in the ongoing moments, consciously observing your thoughts, feelings, and sensations without judgment. This awareness brings you out of the autopilot mode, where you are merely existing and not truly living the moments. Living on autopilot mode renders you prone to functioning unconsciously by relegating your cognitive functions to habitual norms. Here you can't hear the whispers of your thoughts, feelings, and sensations. You become oblivious to the present moment, ultimately missing out experiences that can bring joy, insights, or emotional growth.

Whereas, Mindfulness allows you to detach from habitual impulses, paving the way for a surge in emotional intelligence. As you pay close attention to each emotion as it arises, recognizing its roots and impacts on your body and mind, you foster self-understanding and empathy. Importantly, being stuck on autopilot sets the stage for negativity to thrive. Consumed by past regrets, future anxieties or being entangled in the trials of life, you welcome negative emotions such as stress or fear. On the contrary, mindfulness empowers you to savor the richness of every moment, leaving less room for negative thoughts to take hold.

Mindfulness, when practiced diligently, can help you in the following ways:

1. Brings Clarity: As you transition from autopilot to mindful living, you start acknowledging your thoughts, taking notice of the trivial experiences, realizing the beauty of the present moment, thus inviting clarity into your life.

2. Reduces Stress: By grounding you in the present, mindfulness helps alleviate stress that stems from dwelling in the past or future. It acts as a buffer, cushioning you against the habitual patterns that might lead to stress or anxiety.

3. Enhances Focus: Mindfulness strengthens your focus by continuously drawing your attention away from distracting thoughts back into the present moment.

4. Promotes Empathy: With enhanced self-awareness comes greater empathy. The more attentive you are to your own emotions, the easier it becomes to understand and respond to others' feelings, consequently weaving stronger interpersonal relationships.

5. Fosters Resilience: Mindful individuals tend to be more resilient. They develop the capability to bounce back from challenges as they are more aware of their emotional reactions and can therefore engage in proactive problem-solving.

6. Improves Decision Making: Mindfulness also leads to improved decision-making abilities. It allows you to consider your options with a clear mind, free from the clutches of preconceived notions or biases, thereby paving the way for well-thought-out decisions.

Hence, this seemingly simple shift from autopilot to mindfulness bears significant potential to enrich your life. Adopting the practice of mindfulness is akin to awakening to the magnificence of everyday moments, fostering emotional intelligence, and warding off negativity. So, plunge into the experience of present moment fully, and let mindfulness introduce you to the beauty of life untapped by the mundane rigidity of autopilot living.

At times, society or our deep-seated personal habits may create a hindrance to being fully present in the moment. We are often affected by societal pressures, inner skepticism, and challenging life circumstances that create barriers towards becoming mindful. It is critical to break down these barriers to tap into the power of mindfulness and enrich our lives. The echo of societal pressures has a profound influence on our ideologies and habits. Conformity to societal norms, the urge of staying connected digitally, or maintaining an overflowing work schedule often pulls us away from the quietude of the present. In our pursuit to fit into the prevailing societal norms, we often miss cherishing the tranquility of the present.

One effective technique to combat these societal pressures is to practice daily 'digital detox'. It is an intentional disconnect from screens to reconnect with our inner selves as well as the outside world. Allotting a specific time, during the day for this detox and slowly increasing the duration can be highly effective. Moving onto internal barriers, skepticism or doubt about mindfulness often distracts us. For instance, the thought that mindfulness practices are time-consuming, or need particular settings or skills, often discourages us. However, the core idea is to integrate mindfulness into our everyday activities without any rules or constraints. The best approach to manage inner skepticism is to practice mindfulness in small chunks during the day. Whether washing the dishes, brushing your teeth, or commuting, you can practice mindfulness anywhere, any time. As you progressively practice and experience the benefits, skepticism will gradually fade away.

Another common barrier to mindfulness is our challenging life circumstances. We are so entangled in our daily chores and high-stress environments that we often view mindfulness as an additional task. But rather, mindfulness is designed to weave into our lives seamlessly, dissolving stress. A useful strategy in managing this is to use affirmation techniques. Affirmations are powerful statements that can condition our subconscious mind to develop a positive perspective, thereby reducing stress levels. Regularly reciting affirmations like "I choose to be present right now" or "I am at peace with what is happening right now" help shape our mindset towards mindfulness.

Emotional well-being is deeply connected to mindfulness. It's a vital component in managing stress, fostering well-being, and maintaining healthy relationships. We often fret about the past or are anxious about the future, leading to emotional imbalance. But, bringing our attention to the present moment provides stability and draws us towards a balanced emotional state. Meditative practices go a long way in promoting emotional well-being. Guided meditation, focusing on breath or body sensations help align ourselves with the present, calming our restless minds.

Journal Exercise:

1. Reflect on a specific moment of your day when you were fully present in the situation, not thinking about the future or the past. Write it down in detail.
2. Now think about a moment when you were operating on autopilot - perhaps when you were commuting, brushing your teeth, or doing some household chores. Write it down.
3. Compare both experiences. How did they affect your mood and overall sense of well-being?
4. Based on these reflections, list down three practical steps you can take to incorporate mindfulness into your daily routine. You may consider activities like mindful eating, meditation, or simply spending a few minutes focusing on your breath.

Remember, the goal is not to eliminate all future-minded or automated tasks, but rather to pepper in times of mindfulness throughout the day. Reflect on how this balance may look in your life moving forward.

Learning How to Be Mindful

Whatever your age, there are several things that you can do that will help you to tap into mindfulness so that you can more fully experience the moment. Don't worry – mindfulness isn't like exercising because you don't have to buy anything to practice it. All you need is a quieter place where you can keep your focus. Meditation is the best form of mindfulness, so a lot of these steps will be familiar if you already meditate (or have meditated in the past and have been meaning to go back to it).

The following is what you should do to practice being mindful.

- Find a quiet space where no devices are playing or making noise.
- Sit somewhere in a comfortable place, making sure you are sitting up straight. You want to have your body in a neutral position to provide more support to your back and organs.
- Set a timer of between 5 and 10 minutes, then put it close to you.
- Sit still and focus on your breathing and the feel of your body. Work to remain in the same comfortable position, controlling your breathing as you sit there.
- Pay attention to your thoughts. If they start to stray from the moment, such as thinking about whether or not you sent that email or an issue at work or considering your schedule for tomorrow, stop the thoughts. Put your mind back on the way your body feels and your breathing.

Even the most practiced meditators have wandering minds at some point in time. The point isn't to force yourself into the moment because that will create a negative feeling toward being mindful. You want to help guide your mind to the things you want to think about when it gets off track. What you are doing is paying attention and noticing when you start to drift off from what you want to consider, then to gently refocus yourself.

There's no shaming or self-blaming with being mindful. If you laugh a little because you find you are having trouble with staying focused, that could actually help you. There are going to be times when staying focused is going to be difficult because there is so much happening. Use mindfulness to help you clear out the unnecessary thoughts with the understanding that completely clearing your mind isn't going to be easy. When this happens, you probably don't have 5 or 10 minutes to dedicate to being mindful because you will spend all of that time worrying about the things you *aren't* doing instead. That's ok. It's not a problem if you can't practice mindfulness every day, just like you don't have to vigorously exercise every day. It is good to do it regularly, even years after you learn how to be mindful, because that is the best way to ensure you are more aware. There is a reason for the expression "Use it or lose it," and this is one of those things where you want to make sure that you can continue to be mindful over the rest of your life. It helps you to not only be more positive in your thinking, but also to just enjoy the world around you a bit more. It's much easier to do when you are more frequently present in the moment.

The beauty of mindfulness lies in its non-judgmental nature. When practicing mindfulness, we do not label or evaluate our feelings as 'good' or 'bad'; we merely acknowledge their existence. This non-judgmental observance demystifies our emotions, neutralizing their power over us. Mindfulness allows us to view our feelings from a broader perspective, thereby offering us greater control and flexibility in how we respond to them. For instance, if we encounter a sense of frustration, mindfulness prompts us to recognize and accept it, rather than suppressing or rationalizing it. We learn to understand its origin- be it a specific event or an accumulation of events, thus enabling us to address the genuine root of our frustration rather than the surface-level symptoms.

Other Ways to Practice Being Mindful

There are going to be times when you feel a little too stressed, too energetic, or don't have a quiet place to sit and practice meditation. That's fine. Mindfulness can be done nearly anywhere at any time. In the early days, it will just be much easier to do in a quiet place because you probably aren't accustomed to focusing on your thoughts – most of us aren't. You can practice mindfulness nearly anywhere because it is about being in the moment so that you are more aware. The following are some activities that you can do while you practice being more mindful.

Taking a walk, particularly on a nice day. When it feels good outside, you are going to find it far easier to be present because we naturally appreciate good weather that helps calm us down. The exercise will also help you to keep your focus as moving is one way to get a better handle on your thoughts. When your body is mobile, you tend to be more present, if for no other reason than because survival has taught us to be more careful when we are on the go.

Stop and think about how you feel and what you are thinking if you are sitting or standing around waiting for something or someone. If you are a parent picking your child up from an activity, this is a perfect time to focus on your thoughts because you don't have much else to do that is productive. If you are standing in line, instead of pulling out your phone, consider your thoughts and take in your surroundings. There is a lot going on around you at all times. Many of us are in the habit of pulling out our phones and ending up being upset by social media, emails, or the news. Practicing being mindful will not only help you think more positively, it will help you keep your blood pressure down because you aren't letting the things you can't control get to you.

Take a break a few times a day to stretch, look away from monitors, and think about your current mindset. This is an activity you are probably told to do often by medical professionals, so consider this as being one more time when you are being given permission to stop and be healthy. By forcing yourself to stop and disconnect from work, school, homework, or something else that you have been focusing on, you will have a chance to pay attention to how you are feeling about what is happening. If you are feeling stressed, upset, bothered, angry, or experiencing any negative emotion, you will have a chance to start to adjust those thoughts.

Reflect on your emotions as you prepare for bed. A lot of us have the tendency to replay events from the day, which is usually going to make it harder to sleep. From feeling negative emotions to obsessing over something to trying to make a plan, there is a lot that we do before we go to sleep that actually keeps us from drifting off to sleep. Instead of reflecting on the day or thinking about tomorrow, focus on how you feel. You can focus on how tired you are, helping to calm your mind to sleep. You may also realize that you aren't quite tired enough to sleep, in which case you should get up and do something that will help you get tired enough to sleep. That's killing two birds with one stone since lying in bed trying to get to sleep can create a habit of not being able to go to sleep.

Notice that all of these suggestions end up leading to you being more aware of your emotions as well. Most of them are things that you are likely to do anyway – or things that you have been meaning to do. By starting to practice mindfulness, you will start to become more aware of your emotions and your thoughts, giving you a chance to start understanding more about yourself.

Practice mindfulness several times a day. If possible, jot down notes about what you experienced when you were being mindful. The next chapter is going to focus on emotional intelligence, and being mindful is where you start to understand your emotions. By writing down how you feel at different times of the day or entering a log of what you are thinking about over the course of the day can help you find patterns in your thought process. Ultimately, this is going to be incredibly helpful when you start working on being more positive in your thoughts.

Next to the practical steps from above, integrating mindfulness into everyday activities has been shown to have profound cognitive effects. As a ritualistic practice, it wires the brain to develop neural pathways that foster greater clarity, focus, and attention. Cooking, gardening, and housekeeping, often dismissed as simple chores, can become platforms of mindfulness practice, bringing a wealth of cognitive benefits.

Let's delve into each of these activities:

Cooking: Cooking can be an immersive, multisensory experience that allows us to engage with the present moment. By directing our focus towards each ingredient, we become more attuned to the texture, smell, and color. Every slice, chop, or stir can become an act of meditation, realigning the mind towards a state of calmness and clarity. Consequently, our cognitive abilities to focus and pay attention become sharper.

Gardening: Engaging with the soil and the earth, the feel of the leaves, and the growth of a plant, allow us to connect with nature, thus enhancing our awareness of the world beyond ourselves. This connection grounds us, quieting the mental chatter and expanding our understanding of the interdependent nature of existence, thus enhancing our cognitive ability to perceive the world in an objective, non-judgmental manner.

Housekeeping: Mundane as it might seem, housekeeping is a wonderful exercise in mindfulness. Paying attention to each fold, each sweep, and each rearrangement helps us to stay in the moment. Psychologically, the act of cleaning can also cleanse the mind, promoting cognitive clarity and mental organization.

The cognitive enhancement from these practices holistically interacts with emotional intelligence, a key skill for personal and professional growth. Our cognitive abilities to focus, perceive, and understand infuse emotional intelligence with depth, helping us navigate social scenarios with assertiveness, empathy, and wisdom. Better focus and attention allow us to identify and understand our emotions and those of others more accurately. By being present and mindful in our interactions, we sidestep the pitfalls of knee-jerk reactions and respond in a measured and authentic way. Our cognitive understanding of the interconnectedness of existence, gained through mindfulness exercises like gardening, improves our empathy. We become better at understanding and appreciating the subjective experiences of others, and that enhances our ability to relate to them constructively. Fostering these cognitive effects through mindfulness in daily activities helps enhance emotional intelligence, thereby strengthening personal relationships, boosting productivity at work, and paving the way for overall wellbeing. This offbeat path of cognitive and emotional development shines a new light on mundane chores, enabling us all to lead richer, more mindful lives.

Exploring the realm of mindfulness, there are few practices as powerful as the creative arts. Their profound impact in shaping our mental aura is stimulating and scientifically verified. Painting, writing, music – can alter the course of our thoughts, open paths to positivity and keep negativity at bay.

Artistic endeavors - be they visual, acoustic, or written - respond to our emotional stimuli in a manner unlike anything else. Engaging actively and mindfully in art not only transforms thoughts but also the resonance of emotions inside us.

Diving into the world of painting can awaken the dormant reserve of creativity in us, the colors we smear on canvas reflecting the hue of our emotions. There's a certain liberation that comes from expressing oneself in such a unfiltered, raw way. This activity can help us to live in the moment, appreciate tiny details, and cultivate mindfulness. Our thoughts are steered towards creativity and away from negativity.

Writing, similarly, is a remarkable tool for channeling thoughts and emotions. It gives voice to the silent turmoil inside, helping us understand and process them better. The act of jotting down thoughts, emotions, or maybe even an imaginative story allows us to vent out buried feelings, invites fresh perspectives and stirs a sense of relief. Writing is also a gate to self-discovery, enabling positive thinking by letting us embrace our highlights and flaws.

As for music, it is nothing short of a wonder drug for mental well-being. It touches the deepest corners of our souls, stirring powerful emotions and fostering an atmosphere of peace and tranquility. The rhythm syncs with our heartbeats, the melody pacifies negativity, and lyrics often speak the unspoken. Playing an instrument or simply listening to music can significantly elevate mood and induce positivity.

A fascinating yet lesser-known fact is that engaging in creative arts triggers the release of dopamine in the brain. Dopamine, the feel-good hormone, uplifts mood, boosts positivity, decreases anxiety, and reduces negativity. Practicing art allows us the esoteric luxury to escape the shackles of time and space, transcending to an ethereal state of mindfulness where every brush stroke, every written word, every note played has a symphony to orchestrate in totality.

Engaging in the creative arts is not only an expression of what's within us, it also shapes what goes on within us. As we navigate our lives, mindfulness becomes a necessity. Coloring a canvas, penning down thoughts, or resonating with a melody empowers us to face our thoughts, acknowledge them rather than resisting, and in the process, cultivate positivity. Embracing the arts is an act of self-compassion that opens our minds, unravels our thoughts, clears the mental clutter, and leaves behind a canvas of positivity. Engulfed in the rhythm of creativity, negativity loses its power.

Journal Exercise:

1. Place your hand on your heart and spend a minute sensing your current state of mind and emotion, then write down what you perceive.
2. Recall a scenario when you waited for someone today or in the past. How did you feel during this moment? How might your experience have transformed if you

were fully present?3. Make two separate lists, one containing positive thoughts and the other negative ones, from throughout your day today. Assess each thought - are there patterns, triggers or specific circumstances tied to each?

3. Try one new mindfulness practice from this chapter, whether it's going for a mindful walk or pausing periodically to assess your mindset. Share about your experience in detail. What was challenging? What was rewarding?

4. Before going to bed tonight, take a moment to reflect on your emotions. How did they fluctuate throughout the day and why? How do you feel at the very end, preparing for rest?

5. Reflect on how practicing mindfulness has impacted your emotional intelligence so far. Can you notice any changes in how you perceive, understand, or manage your emotions?

Each night, aim to jot down at least three key points reflecting on the day's experience of practicing mindfulness and emotional awareness. Seek to find the pattern in your emotions and experiences, and how this growing insight is leading you towards growth and better understanding of yourself.

CHAPTER 3

Understanding and Developing Emotional Intelligence

Also known as EQ (meaning emotional quotient, in the same way that intelligence quotient is known as IQ), emotional intelligence refers to a person's ability to understand, process, and manage their own emotions. A person with a high emotional intelligence is able to use their emotions to create positive responses, such as being able to alleviate stress, be more effective in their communication, and to defuse tense situations and conflict. They don't shut down when a difficult topic is brought up, instead they look for ways to discuss the problem in a way that is open, honest, and beneficial to the people involved in the discussion.

While some people have better EQ naturally, everyone can learn to be more attuned to their emotions and learn to use them effectively for a positive outcome. The problem is that people tend to be more accustomed to letting their emotions take control. There are definitely times when that is a survival reaction, such as fear when you freeze, fight, or flee, but most emotions should be processed and worked with, not be the driving force behind your actions.

Of course, this does get harder as you get older if you are used to reacting more emotionally. It will take a good bit of effort to better manage your emotions, but it is essential for you to be able to think positively. If you let your emotions override your thoughts, it will undo whatever work you've done to think more positively.

Emotional intelligence also includes understanding other people and their emotions. That's because you and your relationships are affected just as much by the emotions of others, so you need to be able to understand what they are feeling so that you can react better. For example, if your child is angry after school, you want to talk to your child to help them work through the anger in a way that is positive. Being able to do that will help strengthen your relationship.

The Four Attributes of Emotional Intelligence

Almost all of us could do with a bit more emotional intelligence because the daily grind can wear down patients and our ability to be more emotionally intelligent. To help you better control emotions, even at the end of the day, it will help to understand the four attributes of emotional intelligence to have a better handle on those emotions.

Self-management is exactly what it sounds like; the ability to control your reactions to emotions. This includes following through with commitments and an ability to be adaptable as circumstances change.

Self-awareness is something that most of us have, but we don't practice it as often as we probably should. For emotional intelligence, being self-aware means being able to recognize what you are feeling and how your emotions are affecting your actions. You know what your strengths and weaknesses are, giving you confidence in your response to those emotions.

Social awareness refers to a person's ability to be empathetic with the people around them. You are able to understand the emotions others are feeling and the needs that could help them when they need assistance. This means being able to pick up on other people's emotional cues and understanding the power dynamics in a group setting.

Relationship management is being able to develop and then maintain positive relationships with others. This requires the ability to communicate and positively influence people in those relationships. It helps to be more successful when working in teams and helps to better manage conflict within the group.

You probably already have a basic understanding of most of these attributes, but they have a particular use when it comes to developing better emotional intelligence. Notice that the last two are actually more related to interacting with others, not just about yourself and managing your own emotions. That reflects how essential it is to be able to understand other people's emotions as it is to understand your own.

How Emotional Intelligence Affects You

EQ isn't tied to IQ. In fact, most people think that people with higher IQs tend to be less emotionally intelligent. This isn't always true, despite the fact that Hollywood tends to play up more intelligent people as being less than emotionally intelligent. There really isn't any known relationship between IQ and EQ, so you don't need to worry about one affecting the other.

Both do affect many of the same areas of life though, so you can use them together to improve both. This lets you build up both of them at the same time to improve your life. For example, someone with a high IQ and a low EQ probably isn't going to be as successful in school or at work because they probably won't be able to work well in teams. As an adult, this can be detrimental to a career because people have to work together on projects – most projects are far too big and complex to assign to an individual person. It is much easier to work with someone who has a higher EQ because they will be better at communicating, coordinating, and managing the situation. People with higher EQs actually make good managers because they are more attuned to how their teams are doing and knowing when they should intervene to help mitigate problems, remove blocks, and diffuse emotions that are running high.

Your emotional intelligence actually plays a significant role in your physical health as well. People who don't manage their emotions well are more likely to act in ways that are risky, such as driving recklessly when they are angry (there is a reason why it is called road rage). Being unable to regulate and control emotions can also lead to increased stress, which causes a whole host of known problems. Stress increases your blood pressure, which adversely affects your circulatory system, increasing the risk of a heart attack or stroke. Most people also know that stress negatively affects a person's immune system. What most people don't know about stress is that it can make a person less fertile, and it is known that it ages a person faster. If for no other reason, you want to improve your emotional intelligence so that you can reduce your stress and improve your health.

Similarly, uncontrolled emotions have a negative effect on your mental health. A person who is less regulated emotionally is more likely to suffer from depression and anxiety. By bringing your emotions under better control, you can reduce these problems.

Better EQ also helps to improve your relationships with others. When you are able to better manage your emotions and are more in touch with the reason you are feeling a certain emotion, you can better communicate that to other people. It also helps you to understand why other people feel the way they do. The higher your EQ, the easier it is to develop stronger relationships, both personally and professionally, because it helps to make you a better communicator.

EQ and social intelligence actually are closely related because your EQ directly affects how you socialize with others. Social intelligence refers to a person's ability to understand their relationship with others, understand a person's interests, and being able to feel satisfied by interactions with others. When you are able to understand your relationships, it is easier to communicate and understand the other person's emotions.

When you develop your EQ, it will improve your social intelligence too.

Deeply understanding your emotions is a crucial part of making well-informed, rational decisions. It's not just a matter of identifying your feelings. You need to understand their sources, contemplate their effects, and determine how they influence your thoughts. This process is part of what we call emotional intelligence. As you increase your emotional intelligence, you'll find yourself making more rational and enlightened decisions in your life.

Firstly, emotions often serve as internal signals, alerting us to important information. For example, fear can signal an impending threat, and happiness could suggest that we are on the right path. Such emotional signals, however, can sometimes be misleading or perhaps overly intense due to past experiences or underlying beliefs. This is where the strength of emotional intelligence shines by deciphering if what we're feeling is an accurate response to our environment or a reaction to something from our past. Emotionally intelligent individuals are skilled at distinguishing between these nuances. They are capable of analyzing their feelings, identifying triggers, and taking note of patterns. This skill permits them to ascertain if their emotional responses are legitimate indicators of current situations, or merely habitual reactions stemming from past experiences. With this understanding, they can make decisions informed by an accurate assessment of the present, rather than being led astray by residual emotions from the past.

Secondly, emotionally intelligent people employ their understanding of their emotions to prevent undesirable impulsive decisions. Emotions are powerful, and in the heat of the moment, they can push us towards actions that we might later regret. By recognizing the rise of an emotion and understanding its cause, you gain the precious opportunity to choose your response instead of being carried away by the feeling. You get to pause, look at the situation objectively, and then decide on the best course of action. This is the epitome of rational decision-making, facilitated by high emotional intelligence. Controlling impulsive decisions can be especially useful in heated arguments or negotiations where keeping control over one's emotions often decides the outcome. Instead of reacting out of anger or frustration, emotionally intelligent people opt for rational, thoughtful responses. They keep their emotions in check, ensuring their decisions keep them aligned with their lasting goals and values, instead of getting caught up in the emotional turmoil of the situation.

Lastly, it's vital to remember that emotional intelligence also involves empathy for others' emotions. This can significantly improve your decision-making in all social scenarios. You respond not only to your feelings but also can consider and understand the emotions of others; it helps in predicting the consequences of your actions on others. This helps you in making informed decisions that consider mutual benefits and impact on relationships.

Emotional intelligence creates a fundamental shift in the decision-making process. It equips you with the ability to comprehend your emotions in a refined manner, control impulsive decisions, and promote empathetic responses. The integration of these essential elements aids in achieving a rational, informed decision, ultimately leading to a richer, more fulfilled life experience.

Journal Exercise:

1. Highlight the key points you gathered from the chapter, How Emotional Intelligence Affects You?' and briefly explain why you think they are key.

2. On a scale of 1-10, rate your current level of emotional intelligence (EQ). Explain why you gave this rating and note areas where improvement might be necessary.

3. Reflect on circumstances in which your EQ significantly impacted an outcome (positive or negative). How did it influence your decision-making, relationships, or overall well-being?

4. Consider situations where you demonstrated high EQ and low EQ. What were the consequences of each, and what lessons did you learn?
5. What measures can you take to improve your EQ going forward based on your understanding of the chapter? List at least three action points.
6. Reflect on the importance of EQ in leadership and teamwork. Can you recall any personal experiences reinforcing this theory?
7. How do you believe your EQ affects your physical and mental health? Write down a few instances when your EQ influenced these aspects.
8. Lastly, consider the relationship between EQ and social intelligence. Discuss experiences where your EQ promoted or hindered social relationships and interactions.

Developing Emotional Intelligence

Anyone can improve their EQ, though it does take work since most people tend to be less emotionally aware. The best time to practice being more emotionally intelligent is when it is hardest to, which can make it that much more difficult. When you are feeling overwhelmed and stressed, that is when you want to start to reign in those emotions so that you don't react in a way that is detrimental to yourself or your relationships. Learning how to manage stress in these moments is how you practice emotional awareness and learn to be more emotionally intelligent.

The four components are where you need to focus your attention to improve your EQ.

Self-management is at the top of these aspects because it is the way you start to be more constructive in managing your emotions. Until you can do that, it is nearly impossible to exercise the other three aspects in any way that will be effective. You have to start with managing your own emotions before you can understand what others are feeling. For most people, stress is the primary issue when it comes to self-management since we tend to lose control when we feel overwhelmed. Think about the last time you felt overwhelmed. You probably felt almost completely out of control of your emotions, resulting in tears, anger, or a sense of despair. Self-management helps you to realize when your stress levels are increasing and learn how to best reduce that stress. This is probably familiar as well because this is one of the components of being more self-aware and present in the moment. This is how your EQ really ties into your thought process.

Self-awareness is the next component, with the focus on making sure you don't get to a point where you are feeling overwhelmed. It means being more connected to the way you are feeling and the flow of your emotions into each other. Over the course of the day, most of us experience an entire spectrum of emotions, even if it is only low levels of those emotions. For example, you may feel really annoyed by someone cutting you off while you are driving, acting as a type of low-level anger. Then you hear a joke on the radio that makes you laugh, followed by something that seems to run out in front of your car, but you realize it is just a bag. In the span of 5 minutes, you've felt anger, humor, fear, and relief. Tomorrow, you probably won't even remember most of these emotions because you tend to just let those emotions flow over you without paying much attention to them. Self-awareness means paying attention to those emotions. You don't have to jot down everything you feel or hold onto those emotions. It's simply that you are more aware of them so that you don't get to the point of feeling more stressed or build up negative emotions. Mindfulness is used to improve your self-awareness of emotions.

Social awareness is developed by paying more attention to the people around you, and less time in your head. This means picking up on nonverbal cues to help you communicate with others better. For example, if you are talking to someone and that person starts to back up, this is an obvious sign that they are trying to leave the conversation. Similarly, if they turn their feet away from you and lean away, these are signs that they are not very engaged in the conversation. The best way to address this is to end the conversation and let that person go and take care of something else or talk to someone else. Mindfulness is absolutely essential to being more socially aware because it means paying attention to others.

Relationship management is the last aspect to focus on improving because all of the other aspects will make it easier to manage those relationships naturally. This doesn't mean you won't have some work, to do but you will automatically start to better manage your relationships when you understand your emotions, their causes, and what others are feeling. To improve this aspect you need to work on having better nonverbal communication. Detectives are very good at this part because it helps them when trying to figure out who committed crimes. They are able to do things like mirror someone in an interrogation, naturally building up a better rapport with that person because they are showing a level of connectivity that suggests empathy. You don't need to become that adept at relationship management – unless you want to be a detective – but you do want to be able to read people well enough to be able to introduce humor to reduce stress or to be able to offer support when someone is struggling. That last attribute is particularly important because there is a tendency for people to have a hard time asking for help these days, and it isn't always because they are aware of their problems. Sometimes, a person won't ask for help because they aren't as aware of what they are feeling. Being supportive and helping someone who is less aware can really develop a strong bond with that person. The best thing that can come from relationship management though is the ability to better manage conflict. You can significantly reduce your own stress by being more aware of the dynamics between you and others. Then if there are conflicts, you will be able to act more quickly to diffuse the problem. It won't solve everything, but you can help improve your life overall by being good at diffusing difficult situations.

Applying emotional intelligence in everyday life might not come naturally, but with consistent practice, it becomes second nature. Engage in mindfulness, take responsibility for your feelings, practice empathetic listening, show kindness, respect boundaries, and remember to take a pause when emotions run high. Gradually, you'll notice a positive shift within you and in the way you relate to the world around you, ultimately guiding you towards a path of resilience, self-love, and well-deserved confidence. Emotional intelligence, often, begins at home. The family setting provides the primary platform for emotional learning, with each interaction serving as a mini lesson in emotional articulation. Parents modeling emotional intelligence can instill virtues of empathy, understanding, and emotional self-control in their children. Interactive family activities like shared meals, conversations, or games can serve as opportunities to promote empathy, patience, and emotional awareness, ultimately leading to better conflict resolution skills and emotional maturity among family members. Moving to the workplace, emotional intelligence becomes pivotal. The employees and leaders high in emotional intelligence can navigate through interpersonal relations smoothly, helping to foster a positive and productive work environment. It aids in understanding and managing the emotions of team members, fostering empathy, and enhancing communication. This results in low-conflict and high-motivation settings where everyone feels valued and understood. Training programs can be employed to improve emotional intelligence among employees, enhancing their job satisfaction, performance, and interpersonal relationships, making the workplace an enjoyable rather than stressful environment.

At a larger scale, emotional intelligence within community settings paves way for harmonious cohabitation. Communities high in collective emotional intelligence enjoy healthier interpersonal relationships, with fewer cases of misunderstanding, prejudice, or conflict. Emotional intelligence fosters inclusivity; urging community members to empathize with diverse types of people, lifestyles, cultures, and beliefs. Engaging in community services, clubs, or group activities can provide ample opportunity to harness and exercise emotional intelligence within an individual.

Journal Exercise:

1. Identify a recent moment where your emotions felt overwhelming. What strategies did you use to deal with it? Could any component of EQ (Emotional Intelligence) have been applicable in that situation?

2. Reflect on these four components of EQ: Self-management, Self-awareness, Social awareness, and Relationship management. Rate yourself on a scale of 1-10 on each component. Explain your rating and outline specific steps on how you could improve in each area.

3. Think about a recent conversation you had with someone. Were you fully present and mindful of non-verbal cues? How could increased social awareness have changed the interaction?

4. Recall a recent conflict you experienced. How did you respond? What was the outcome? Can you think of strategies within the domain of Relationship management that could have affected the outcome differently?

5. Over the next week, make a conscious effort to monitor and introspect on your emotions at three specific times each day. What patterns do you see? Is there a correlation between different times, activities, and shifts in your emotions?

6. At the end of the week, conduct an overview. How far have you come in terms of your emotional intelligence? Reflect on the changes you've noticed in your personal well-being and interactions with others from your efforts to improve your EQ.

CHAPTER 4

Understanding Your Own Mindset

You've learned a lot so far, but for the most part, it has been more about informing you than in helping you actually start shifting your thought process. That's because you need all of the details to start making changes. Now there is one thing left you need to do before you can start thinking more positively.

Now, you need to find your thinking baseline. You may feel you already know if you are an optimistic or pessimistic person, but that's still not quite the same thing. Also, no one is completely one or the other. That's exactly what this chapter is about – learning more about your own way of thinking.

It's important to understand that over the course of a day, your mindset is going to change. When you are feeling good, it is much easier to think positively, and when you are feeling down you are more likely to have negative thoughts. While you don't need to track those thoughts just yet, it is important to realize that how you think at different points in time is going to be just as critical as understanding your overall mindset. After all, when you are already thinking positively, you aren't going to need to adjust it. At the same time, you shouldn't rest on your laurels with the belief that you are making progress without actively working against negative thoughts when they arise.

The Repetitive Nature of Thinking

While emotions and events will affect your thinking, we tend to follow similar thought patterns. Even when we experience something new, we are more likely to experience repetitive thinking, with people who tend to think about the future letting their thoughts drift into what ifs, and people who focus on the past tending to compare their new experience with something in their past. Both of these attitudes fail to reflect the moment in favor of the repetitive thinking that we are accustomed to following. It's not something we do knowingly, but as a part of our thinking habits.

Since a lot of our thoughts are done without much awareness, you need to understand what your repetitive thought patterns are to have an understanding of what you are more inclined to think when something happens.

Our established thought patterns are subconscious – your job is to make that pattern conscious so that you can start examining and altering it. Considering how many thoughts you have every day, you are going to quickly have a very large sample size of what your patterns are within a few weeks. The problem is that you aren't going to be aware every waking moment, and over time, you are more likely to become less focused on your thoughts as you slip back into old habits. You don't need to be constantly aware, but you will need to actively work to understand your thought patterns so that the negativity isn't able to slip into your thinking without being challenged or questioned.

As you start to become more aware of your own thought patterns, some of your emotions are going to start making more sense. When negative thoughts move from your conscious thoughts into your subconscious thoughts, it creates a habit of negative beliefs that generate negative emotions without you even being aware that this is where your negative feelings are rooted.

To become more aware of your thoughts, here are some exercises you can start doing a couple of times a day.

- Think of your thoughts as being separate from yourself. Since we are more likely to be aware of our surroundings, considering your thoughts as being an outside influence will help to make you more aware of those thoughts. Your thoughts are not even constant, and as you know if you have ever walked into a room and forgotten why you are there, thoughts are just temporary. It's when you start paying more attention to them that they begin to mean more, and you can start to change them.

- When you have time, actively think about what you are thinking. It sounds impossible, but even that is a thought you are currently having. And now you are probably starting to get into your own head because every line you read inspires another thought. What you need to do is to be more aware of these thoughts when you have time. For example, when you are sitting at home and relaxing, focus on the thoughts passing through your head. This can be when you are watching TV or doing something passive. Or maybe you are cooking or cleaning, in which case your mind is definitely running wild with a range of thoughts. This is the perfect opportunity to really know what you are thinking. You can also do this while stuck in traffic, but don't get so lost in paying attention to your thoughts that you forget to pay attention while you are driving. This is an exercise to do when you aren't doing something that requires your attention; it is more of an activity to do when you are bored or doing something when you are likely to put your mind on autopilot. You will get a rich set of thoughts that more accurately reflect your thought patterns when you tap into your mind when it is left largely to its own devices rather than trying to steer it in one direction or another.

- Be careful not to put too much emphasis into any single thought. You need to take them lightly. Negative thoughts are going to float through your mind because it's bound to happen. Then you are bound to get some really random thoughts that leave you questioning yourself. Usually, this is a result of boredom or a desire to think something different. Imagination is fantastic, and as long as your thoughts are driving you to do something illegal or unethical, it's just a passing thought. Encourage your mind to move toward something more imaginative. You are controlling the thoughts, at least partially, and seeing where they go. There are few better ways to get an idea of your thought patterns than to give them free reign to better understand what kinds of events and ideas your mind is drawn to. When it comes time to start trying to steer your thoughts, it will be much easier if you know how you arrive at certain types of thoughts.

Take the time to consider the kinds of thoughts you've had and how they affect you. Have an idea of what thoughts lead to negativity and negative emotions, and what causes more positive thoughts and positive feelings.

Split Thoughts up According to Helpful and Limiting

There are actually a lot of classifications you can give them, including negative and positive. Make it something fun so that you are more likely to keep going with the exercise. It is probably best not to use terms like angel and devil since you don't literally demonize your thoughts. They are just thoughts – nothing permanent. The goal is to work toward naming thoughts that help and those that harm you. The thoughts themselves aren't the problem, but the pattern that encourages negative thoughts and emotions. At best, they are friends and foes, but even that might be a little too much since it can make you feel like your thoughts are working against you – and no one needs to feel like their mind is actively working to undermine them.

While you are doing an activity that doesn't really occupy your mind, pay attention to what you are thinking. Start to analyze that thought to determine if it is helpful to your mindset, emotions, or situation, or if it is something that feels more harmful or not helpful.

- It's positive that what you are thinking is simply nonsensical, in which case, you can just let that thought go on its merry way, potentially noting it as inspirational for any creative activities that you enjoy. No one said you had to be asleep and dreaming to have thoughts that leave you wondering what is going on with your mind.

- If the thought is positive, take the time to appreciate it because it's probably boosting your emotions in a way that is positive. Give yourself a moment to feel happy about it – giving yourself two positive boosts at once.

- If the thought is negative or not helpful, stop and consider why you had it. It could be a part of your thought pattern, either about the subject, because of your current mood, or just a general negative stream of thoughts. Don't dwell on it or overanalyze it because it was literally just a passing thought. There was no intention by your thought process to harm you, just something passing through and that shouldn't be considered a problem on its own. Only a steady, long-term stream of negative thoughts is going to be harmful.

This should be a fun exercise that literally gives you insight into your own mind. Even though you've lived with yourself every day up to this point in your life, your mind and thoughts are probably as much a mystery to you as they are to the people around you. Keep the process entertaining, generating some positive emotions around it so that you will be able to keep doing it, learning about your thoughts whenever you do it.

If you can do this at least once a day, you will get a better idea of how you think. If you set aside 5 to 10 minutes a couple of times a day to do this exercise, you will understand your mindset and thought process a lot faster. You should still continue to do this over the years because it is just nice to know what you are thinking, even if you don't exactly know why. It can give you insight into your emotions, as well as help you better understand if a situation is bothering you. You shouldn't be making major decisions based on this exercise that's meant to be fun, but if you notice that you keep having negative thoughts around work, a particular event, or a certain aspect of your life, it could indicate that you need to start considering changes, or at least talking to people to see if you can improve the situation.

This exercise is also great for keeping emotions in check. If you feel stressed, overwhelmed, or have any negative emotion, and if you can take time out to run through the process, you may understand why you feel the way you do. It can also help you notice if you are starting to feel anxious or depressed. It isn't a replacement for consulting a professional, but this exercise can give you a much better understanding of your thoughts and how they affect your emotions, as well as how your emotions may be influencing your thoughts.

CHAPTER 5

Easy Actions to Increase Positive Thinking

There are a lot of ways to start introducing positive thoughts into your daily life, and some of them will work wonders for you and others may not work at all. Everyone is different, so ultimately, you have to find what works for you. This chapter provides a wide range of suggestions you can start implementing to put more positivity into your thought process, even if you are still working through your own assessment of the way you think.

The point of this chapter is to start adding more positivity into your thought process, regardless of whether you are optimistic, pessimistic, realistic, or something else. Being able to add some positivity into your thoughts will benefit you because you are bound to have times when positivity is far more difficult to achieve. When you are highly stressed, feeling depressed, or are dealing with a serious situation, there are many reasons why you are going to feel negative emotions – even if you are a very positive person.

Take the time to try out all of these different methods to see which ones work for you. It's possible that some ideas will work better than others when you are in a particular mental state. For example, some of these methods may work better when you are upset than when you are bored or busy. Some may prove to be beneficial before you go to sleep or when you first wake up. You may find that some methods are even more effective later in your life. Just because a suggestion doesn't work the first couple of times doesn't mean that it won't ever work. You have to find the right solutions for different situations, mental states, and periods of the day. The important part is finding the methods that work when you need them so that you can keep some positivity going for the rest of your life.

Your Daily Affirmations

This is idea that most of us write off because it seems hokey at best and a waste of time at worst. However, if you pay attention to your thoughts, you are probably already talking about yourself, even if you don't say it aloud. There is a chance that you are putting yourself down when you do this. Daily affirmations aren't about being conceited, but about pointing out that you are capable.

Starting the day with positive affirmations can help to set a positive tone for the rest of the day. You don't have to say the things that you've heard in TV shows or the stereotypical daily affirmations either. You can come up with your own affirmations that help to make you feel better about your day. Remember, being positive isn't about faking it until you make it. You are supposed to say things that make you feel positive. The following are some typical affirmations, and then a few more unique ones.

- "I am good enough."
- "I can do anything I put my mind to doing."
- "I can make good decisions, and I will choose to make good decisions today."
- "I am happy and healthy."
- "It's a new day, and I'm going to make sure to enjoy it."
- "I'm in charge of my life."

- "I am the protagonist in my story."
- "I can create the change I want in my life."
- "I will make my own choices, not wait to be chosen."
- "I messed up yesterday, but I have learned my lesson. Today will be better."
- "Life may not be perfect, but I'm going to make today as close to perfect as possible."
- "I want to be more adventurous, and I'm starting today."
- "I'm not going to compare my life to that of strangers online because I'm going to focus on making my life fantastic on its own."
- "I can't wait to see what today will bring."

You can make your own positive sayings too. As long as you are telling yourself something positive about your day, yourself, or your situation, it's a positive affirmation that can help you. That's probably why so many people think that positive thoughts are so hokey, they aren't tailored to what you need to boost your spirits and set a positive expectation for the day.

A fresh, customized perspective can transform the effectiveness of your affirmations; crafting personal affirmations allows them to resonate more deeply and become a powerful tool. Let's explore some ways to create these nuggets of positivity and how to incorporate them into your everyday life.

The first method to create a personalized affirmation is to make it strikingly specific. A generic affirmation such as "I am successful" has its place, but specifying what success means to you can make it more potent. Visualize a specific aspect of your life you wish to improve or a particular goal you want to achieve. Embed this image in your affirmation. For instance, “I am a splendid public speaker who engages and inspires her audience” will probably have more meaningful implications for someone trying to improve communication skills.

Another method to personalizing your affirmations is to incorporate your core values. Reflect on the principles that you hold dear: it could be love, integrity, kindness, or peace. Use these to guide your affirmations. For instance, “I tirelessly embody kindness and compassion in my interactions with others”. Such an affirmation is rooted in your values, making it more personal and therefore more influential.

Emotion is the spice of life; infuse it in your affirmations. Personalize your affirmations by including emotions you wish to feel. Positive affirmations are a vessel to carry you to your desired emotional state. If you want to feel loved, an affirmation could be “I am enveloped by love and affection everywhere I go”.

Also, weave in your unique strengths and capabilities into your affirmations. It enforces a positive self-image and reinforces your belief in yourself. If you are exceptional in painting or softball, make that a part of your affirmation.

Now the crucial part - integrating these personalized affirmations into your daily routine. Consistency is key for these affirmations to take root and influence your thought process.

1. Start your day with affirmations: Begin your morning by repeating your affirmations. It sets a positive tone for the day and mentally prepares you for what lies ahead.

2. Leverage technology: Set alerts on your phone to remind you to repeat your affirmations. There are also several apps available that can aid in incorporating affirmation practice into your daily schedule.

3. Merge them into your mindfulness practice: If meditation, yoga, or any mindfulness exercise is a

part of your routine, incorporate your affirmations into them. The tranquil environment will help it seep deeper into your conscious and subconscious mind.

4. Affirmative notes: Writing your affirmations on sticky notes and placing them around your home or workspace can serve as constant reminders. Every glance towards it sears the affirmation deeper into your psyche.

5. Bedtime affirmation: Repeat your affirmations before you sleep. During sleep, our subconscious mind is at the forefront, absorbing and processing the information from the whole day. Supplying it with positive affirmations can work wonders.

Never forget, the strength of affirmations lie not in their repetition alone, but in the belief behind them. Believe in your affirmations and watch as they bring positive change into your life, one thought at a time. Start small, with a single specific affirmation and then expand your repository as you become comfortable with the process. Your brain then acts upon this new narrative, shaping your reality to fit your beliefs. This adaptive cognitive process is what we refer to as cognitive restructuring. Cognitive restructuring, a cornerstone in cognitive behavioral therapy (CBT), is the process of challenging, and ultimately changing, distorted thoughts or negative patterns of thinking, replacing them with more positive, realistic thoughts. Through affirmations, you're actively engaging in cognitive restructuring, debunking negative thoughts, distorting your interpretation of events, and replacing these with more positive, constructive interpretations.

At the heart of all these processes is the overwhelming task of overcoming negativity. This is no easy feat, given that humans have a natural tendency - a negativity bias - to remember and dwell on negative experiences over positive ones. Studies have shown that it takes about five positive experiences to counterbalance one negative experience. This is where affirmations play an important part. They provide a steady stream of positivity that gradually chips away at the negativity ingrained in our minds, tipping the balance in favor of positivity.

Affirmations work by harnessing the power of neuroplasticity – the brain's ability to reorganize itself by creating new neuron connections. As you repeat positive affirmations, your brain forms fresh clusters of positive-thought neurons replacing old clusters of negative-thought neurons. This is akin to forging a new, sunlit path in a dense jungle, a path that eventually becomes your default, as you consistently choose it over the shadowy, negative one. Thus, every time you affirm yourself positively, you're directly discourse with your subconscious - displacing the old, challenging the distorted, and installing a refreshing perspective. The processes of self-perception and cognitive restructuring, coupled with the inherent resilience to overcome negativity, all work behind the scenes to make affirmations effective.

So, the next time you find yourself amidst self-doubt or negativity, remember that you have the power to influence your reality. Pick a positive affirmation, repeat it to yourself – believe it, and watch as the power of your mind works its magic, restructuring your cognitive landscape, shaping your self-perception and slowly lifting you out of the doldrums of negativity. Become the architect of your mind and the co-author of your life story. Believe in your affirmations, believe in yourself. Remember, the language you use to communicate with yourself matters tremendously. Be your own alchemist; transform mere words into golden positive affirmations that enrich your mind, soothe your soul, and elevate your life. You have within you, the power to nurture a potent inner dialogue – one affirmation at a time.

Journal Exercise:

1. List down the top three positive affirmations you encounter today. Reflect on how these affirmations resonate with you and your personal needs and aspirations.

2. Think about any moment today where you exercise these affirmations. Write down how you felt during and after this moment.
3. Now create your own set of 3 personalized affirmations based on your specific needs and aspirations. How do they differ from the common affirmations?
4. Identify which areas of life (e.g. personal, social, career) each of these affirmations cater to.
5. For each personalized affirmation, write down a short action plan on how you will incorporate them into your daily routine for a more resonant and effective impact.
6. At the end of this exercise, reflect on your feelings. Has your mindset shifted towards a more positive direction as a result of this activity? If so, how? If not, what might be holding you back?

Your progress will build with time. This exercise isn't about immediate, drastic change; rather, it's about cultivating a gradual, positive shift in your mindset and in your daily routines.

Make Time to Meditate

Meditating several times a week (every day if you can swing it, but at least a few times every week) helps you to focus and be mindful. If you start your day with a positive affirmation, you can help settle yourself down with meditation at the other end. It will help you get your thoughts under control, and calm your emotions. Guide your thoughts to more positive aspects of the day or to positive emotions. After a bad day, focus on the things that went right, no matter how small they are. No day is all bad. While you are meditating, you can pay attention to the things that went right because odds are you overlooked them and focused on what went wrong.

It's important to understand that meditation doesn't immediately flip the switch to everlasting positivity. It is a gradual process that requires consistent effort. However, the undeniable effect it produces over time truly proves its worth in ushering in an era of enhanced positivity and mental well-being in one's life.

Commencing an effective meditation routine requires careful planning and consistent dedication. Here is a detailed guide on how you can start:

The initial phase would be to secure a time and place for meditation. It must be a time when you are least likely to be disturbed and a place where you can feel at ease. While early morning works well for many, you need to find a time that suits your routine. As for the location, it could be any spot where you feel composed – be it an idyllic corner of your house or the serenity of a park.

1. Once you have decided the timing and location, proceed by setting an achievable initial goal. Begin with just two minutes a day. Once you get accustomed to meditating, you can gradually increase the duration. It is about consistency rather than duration.

2. One effective technique for beginners is to focus on breathe. Sit comfortably, close your eyes gently and focus your attention on the inhalation and exhalation. You may find your mind straying, it's normal. Gently bring back your attention to your breathing.

3. You can integrate mindfulness into your routine by focusing on routine activities like brushing your teeth or having your breakfast. Be fully present at the moment, savor every bite, every sensation.

4. Walking meditation is another technique that serves dual purpose of physical activity and mental calm. Concentrate on your strides, feel your feet touching the ground. Allow your thoughts to pass without judgment.

5. Contemplation on positive affirmations encourages positivity. Start with simple affirmations like - „I am enough", „I am grateful", or „I am at peace" and silently repeat them during your meditation.

6. As you progress, using guided meditations can be beneficial. They guide you verbally through various stages of meditation and are available in many forms such as apps and online videos.

7. Remember, there is no right or wrong way to meditate. Do what feels comfortable to you. Every experience is a learning experience in the meditative journey. Recognize and accept them.

8. Keep a journal to track your progress. Note down your experiences post meditation, any challenges faced and how you feel throughout the day. It helps in understanding patterns and working on them.

9. Incorporate yoga or light stretching before meditation. It preps you for a calming experience and frees you from physical discomfort which might disrupt your session.

Most importantly, be patient. Meditation is not a quick-fix but a journey. It takes time to train your mind to focus and redirect thoughts but the benefits are substantial. Do not beat yourself up if progress seems slow. Approach meditation with an open heart and mind. The tranquility and awareness that follow are worth the perseverance. Soon, you will find your thoughts having less control over you and that you can live your life more mindfully and effectively.

Journal Exercise:

Begin with a simple mindfulness meditation, clearing your mind of any thoughts and focus on your breath. After your meditation session, grab your journal and answer the following reflection questions:

1. Record your immediate feelings post-meditation. How do you feel, physically and emotionally?
2. Did any thoughts come to mind during meditation? If so, jot them down.
3. Reflect on positive affirmations for your day. What positive thoughts would you like to dominate your day?
4. Consider the challenges of your day and write how these have contributed to your personal growth.
5. What things went well today? It can be anything, however small it might seem.
6. How will you use meditation in the future to help control your thoughts and emotions better?
7. How has your perception of your day changed after meditation and focusing on the positive?

The goal is to develop a positive mindset by paying attention to the good in every situation. Keep this journal handy, to revisit these tasks and keep track of your progress over time.

Think of Three Positives

When you catch yourself thinking negatively, follow it up with three positive thoughts. We humans have a strange habit of focusing on the negative things that have occurred, so you are going to find those without having to really look. We are far less likely to think about the things that have gone right and the positives in our lives.

You probably aren't going to notice all of your negative thoughts, especially when you are unhappy or stressed. This isn't an exercise in monitoring your thoughts, but in making sure you react in a positive way when you notice those negative thoughts. Over time, you'll retrain your brain to react to negativity in a way that will counter it.

The simple act of redirecting negative thoughts by thinking of three positives is transformative. To elevate this practice and anchor it deeply into our daily lives, introducing "Positive Thought Journaling" can be a game-changer. This method combines the act of recognition with the therapeutic process of writing, creating a powerful tool in your positivity arsenal.

Why Journaling?

Writing is a cathartic experience. When we pen down our thoughts, feelings, and experiences, it allows us to confront and process them. This action translates abstract thoughts into something tangible and visible. As with the age-old advice of writing down dreams to remember them better, jotting down positive thoughts makes them more real and memorable.

Setting Up Your Positive Thought Journal

Choosing the Right Journal: Find a notebook or journal that resonates with you. It could be a leather-bound tome, a simple spiral notebook, or even a digital app. What's crucial is that it feels right and invites you to open it.

Creating a Safe Space: Designate a peaceful spot in your home for this activity. This space should be free from distractions and allow you to feel at ease, making the process of journaling a tranquil experience.

Setting Aside Time: While the primary goal is to write when you catch a negative thought, it can also be beneficial to allocate a specific time each day to reflect and write. It could be in the early hours of the morning, during a midday break, or right before bed.

The Journaling Process

Begin by writing the date at the top of the page. Start with the negative thought that you caught yourself thinking. This isn't to dwell on it but to acknowledge it. Once you've written it down, take a deep breath, release it, and then proceed to list three positive thoughts. These could be in direct contrast to the negative thought, or they might be entirely unrelated positive reflections from your day.

For instance, if the negative thought was, "I failed to complete my tasks today," your three positive counter thoughts could be:

- "I managed to prioritize and finish the most crucial task."
- "I had a lovely conversation with a colleague."
- "I enjoyed a delicious lunch."

As you jot down these positive notes, ensure you genuinely feel and internalize them. This practice isn't about superficially masking negativity but about genuinely shifting focus.

Benefits Over Time

In the initial days, you might feel that you're artificially creating positive thoughts, or you might struggle to come up with three. But as with any skill, practice makes perfect. Over time, two things will happen:

Building Positivity Reservoirs: The more you engage in this activity, the easier it will be to recall positive experiences. You'll essentially be building a reservoir of positivity that you can tap into at any time.

Tangible Evidence: On particularly challenging days, flipping through previous pages of your journal serves as a powerful reminder in your life. Each entry stands as evidence of your resilience and the good moments that exist amidst challenges.

Reduced Emphasis on Negativity: As you continue with this journaling journey, you'll notice a diminishing emphasis on the negative thoughts you start with. Over time, the positive notes will dominate your pages, and the negatives will merely be brief, fleeting mentions. This transition isn't just on paper but reflects the transformation occurring in your mindset.

Increased Awareness: By routinely identifying and challenging negative thoughts, you cultivate a heightened sense of awareness. You begin to recognize patterns in your thinking, understanding the triggers for negativity, and are better equipped to preemptively counter them with positivity.

Making It A Shared Experience

Consider sharing this practice with a close friend or family member. Not only does this create a sense of accountability, but it also allows for mutual encouragement. You can share your positive notes with each other, further amplifying the good feelings. Hearing someone else's positive thoughts can often bring joy and offer a different perspective on your own situations.

Cherishing the Evolution

As months go by, don't just let your journal gather dust. Take time, maybe once a month or every few months, to revisit your entries. You'll be surprised to witness your evolution. Some negative thoughts that seemed monumental at the time may now seem trivial in the face of the positives you've amassed. This retrospective view serves as a testament to your growth and the efficacy of the practice.

Positive Thought Journaling isn't just about documenting moments; it's about crafting a narrative of hope, resilience, and joy. It reminds you that while negativity might be an inevitable part of life, so is positivity. It's a choice you make every day, and with this journal, you have a tangible roadmap guiding you towards a more optimistic outlook on life. So, the next time you catch a negative thought, reach out for your journal, and let the transformation unfold, one positive note at a time.

Every day, our senses are bombarded with stimuli that can evoke a multitude of emotions. The scent of a particular perfume might remind you of a cherished person, while a song on the radio could transport you back to a memorable event in your past. Such reactions stem from our brain's remarkable ability to associate stimuli with memories, emotions, or experiences. By understanding and harnessing the power of association, we can actively create positive triggers to counteract negativity.

Understanding Associations and Triggers: At its core, an association is a link formed between two pieces of information in our minds. Over time, with repeated exposure, these links strengthen, allowing for automatic responses. For instance, if you constantly associate a specific song with a happy memory, hearing that tune can instantly elevate your mood.

Creating Positive Associations: While many associations form naturally over time, we possess the power to intentionally create them. Begin by identifying stimuli that can easily be integrated into your daily routine – a specific fragrance, a unique ringtone, a piece of jewelry, or even a visual cue like a picture. Next, deliberately associate that stimulus with a positive experience or emotion. This might mean wearing a specific perfume during happy occasions or playing a certain song whenever you're feeling upbeat. With repeated exposure, the chosen stimulus will start evoking positivity.

Employing Positive Triggers During Negativity: Once you've successfully created a positive association, use it as a tool to combat negative thoughts. If you catch yourself spiraling into a pit of negativity, engage with your positive trigger. Spritz on that perfume, play the song, or glance at the chosen picture. The strong positive association will act as a counterbalance, pulling you out of the negative vortex.

Reinforcing the Association: It's essential to ensure that your positive associations remain potent. This requires periodic reinforcement. Engage with your chosen stimulus during moments of joy, happiness, or achievement. By doing so, you strengthen the link between the stimulus and positivity, ensuring it remains an effective tool against negativity.

Expanding Your Positive Triggers: Don't limit yourself to just one association. Over time, curate a collection of positive triggers. Having an arsenal at your disposal means you can rotate them, preventing any single one from losing its potency due to overexposure. Furthermore, different triggers can be more effective for various types of negativity or situations. A song might lift your spirits when you're feeling blue, but a visual cue like a cherished photograph could be more effective when you're feeling anxious.

Sharing the Experience: Just as with the Positive Thought Journaling, involving friends or family can amplify the benefits. Share your positive triggers with loved ones and encourage them to create their own. When they're feeling down, you can engage their triggers for them, offering comfort and support. Additionally, understanding each other's triggers can foster deeper connections and mutual support.

The Bigger Picture: Associations and triggers aren't just about combating sporadic negative thoughts. They play a role in shaping your overall outlook towards life. By continuously steering your mind towards positivity, you're not just addressing isolated instances of negativity; you're cultivating a more optimistic, positive perspective on life in general.

The world around us is a treasure trove of potential positive triggers. Every scent, sound, and sight holds the promise of becoming a beacon of positivity. It's up to us to identify them, imbue them with positive associations, and then employ them as tools to ward off negativity. Remember, the power of association is potent. Just as Pavlov's dogs learned to associate the sound of a bell with food, you too can train your mind to associate specific stimuli with positivity. So, embark on this exciting journey of discovery and let every day be filled with countless moments of joy, buoyed by the triggers you've thoughtfully created and nurtured.

For the next part, answer the following questions:

1. How did it feel to switch your thoughts from negative to positive?
2. What was difficult about this process?
3. What strategies will you utilize in the future to aid in this changeover whenever negative thoughts arise?
4. How can you ensure you practice this behavior regularly, to help retrain your brain from negativity to positivity?
5. Reflect on the benefits you experienced after this exercise. Can you see anticipated benefits of maintaining this practice over time?

Best Case Scenario

This is something you can do while you are journaling or as you are stuck in traffic. Often our minds wander to topics that are less than positive because we are feeling negatively when we are stuck in traffic or doing a task we don't enjoy. This can lead to people considering worst case scenarios. If you think back, even you can probably think of a time when you've done this, thinking that it would prepare you for the worst to come.

When you find yourself feeling upset, bored, frustrated, or just with time on your hands, take some time to consider the best-case scenarios. This doesn't mean go nuts and think about winning the lottery. This is about thinking about the best-case scenario for the events in front of you. Just like you don't go thinking about an asteroid hitting the planet when considering the worst-case scenario for a promotion you want for work, you don't think about winning the lottery to make the promotion irrelevant. Instead focus on what your best-case scenario for what could happen if you get the promotion, from saving for a house, marriage, or vacation. Keep it realistic and within the bounds of what *you* can make happen, not luck. Save that kind of thinking for daydreaming and stories. A best case scenario is meant to help you see how your actions can help to make positive things happen.

Visualizing positive outcomes is not simply a process of wishful thinking or idle dream exploration. It's a scientifically recognized method of stress reduction and goal achievement. Neuroscience research has shown that by visualizing activities, experiences, or outcomes, the brain triggers the same neural networks as it would if the individual were truly experiencing said activities. There is a blurring of the line between imagined actions and real actions to the brain, and that is the magic behind the power of visualization. To put it scientifically – our brains are inherently incapable of distinguishing the difference between visualizing an event and experiencing it in reality. The mental rehearsal of an action stimulates the same neural pathways that are activated when physically performing that action. This means that our thoughts and visualizations can impact our physical state and emotions, leading on to dramatically influence our attitude and actions. Whether it is a sportsperson visualizing the perfect shot, a musician imagining a flawless performance, or an entrepreneur envisaging success, it all boils down to activating the right neural structures.

Practically speaking, this concept holds immense power in boosting self-confidence and shaping destinies. When you see yourself achieving something in your mind's eye, the image leaves a profound imprint on your subconscious mind. This visual imprint enhances your self-confidence, motivates you to work harder, and subtly influences all your actions towards the realization of that positive outcome. The results may not be immediate, but they're indeed far-reaching. Incorporating visualization into your everyday routine doesn't require enormous effort or time. Here are some simple, effective practices:

1. Take a few minutes every day, preferably in a quiet and relaxing environment, and close your eyes. Picture the best possible outcome of your day, a work assignment, or a life goal in as many details as possible. Really soak in the feeling of achievement.

2. Use all your senses during the visualization. Try to invoke the sounds, smells, tastes, and tactile experiences associated with the positive outcome. A more multi-sensory approach leads to a more immersive and effective visualization.

3. Combine visualization with affirmations. This duo can catalyze your journey towards positivity and success. While visualizing, simultaneously affirm your ability to achieve the visualized outcome. This will not just help your subconscious buy-in but also infuse you with high levels of motivation and resilience.

4. Begin with short-term, smaller goals. As you get better with the practice and start seeing results, move on to visualizing more challenging, long-term goals. This progressive approach will keep your confidence and motivation levels high.

5. Finally, remember to stay consistent with your practice. Just like a physical workout, the benefits of visualization accrue over time. It becomes more effective the more you do it. So, although it is perfectly fine to miss a day or two, make sure you are regularly dedicating time to this powerful practice for the best results.

When assessing the science behind visualization and how it influences attitude and actions, it's crucial to keep in mind that it's not a stand-alone solution. Visualization is a powerful aid but should work in tandem with proactive actions, hard work, and a positive mindset. To capitalize on the strengths of both optimism and realism, it's about cultivating a mindset that allows you to embody both - Optimistic Realism. This leans on the idea that optimism and realism don't need to be mutually exclusive, but rather can coalesce into a potent mindset that can navigate uncertain waters with resiliency.

The journey towards optimistic realism starts with the conscious recognition of the delicate balance needed between these two perspectives. Instead of achieving extremes, aim towards adopting a mid-way path. It's about accepting life's unfavorable realities while at the same time remaining hopeful about the future, the mixture of these two views makes an individual more resilient and adaptable to life's challenges. A crucial aspect of nurturing this mindset lies in practicing mindful awareness. Noting your thought patterns is vital. You may notice that you lean towards either optimism or realism in different parts of your life. This awareness then sets the foundation for ushering in change.

1. Identify Reality: Start by objectively evaluating your current situation. Distinguish the aspects within your control from those outside of it, and allocate your efforts accordingly.

2. Cultivate Hope: Once you've established your reality, instill hope and positivity about your future. Goals set, irrespective of their magnitude, breeds optimism.

3. Rational Steps: Realism ensures the steps towards these goals are rational and achievable, increasing the likelihood of success.

Better mental health and well-being is one of the many dividends of optimistic realism. The acquisition of this balanced perspective helps to reduce the toll of psychological stress and enhances our ability to bounce back from unfortunate circumstances. Instead of being hopelessly crushed by setbacks, optimistic realism allows for resilience, the understanding that obstacles are transient and that better opportunities lie ahead. This understanding negates the formation of mental health complications like anxiety and depression. It allows you to see beyond the immediate problem to focus on potential solutions, creating a buffer for well-being and a base for happiness.

Journal Exercise:

1. Identify a situation you recently faced where you experienced negative thoughts. Describe this situation in detail.
2. Recall the negative thoughts or outcomes you had envisioned in this situation. Write them down.
3. Now, rethink this scenario, replacing those negative thoughts with optimistic and realistic possibilities. What are the best-case scenarios that could have happened?
4. Reflect on what actions you could have taken to contribute to these positive outcomes. Would this have changed your approach to the situation?
5. Based on this chapter, how will you approach similar situations in the future? Write down actionable steps to focus more on positive thinking and visualization.

Practice Positive Lessons from Failure

When we fail at something, it is so easy to let that end up in a downward spiral into endless negative thoughts. However, almost every successful person has experienced a lot of failures in their lives – with Walt Disney being one of the go-to examples of someone who continually failed until he succeeded. Failure is a unique opportunity to learn a lot about what happened, why, and how you can change what you did to increase the odds of success.

Perhaps one of the best examples of failing and learning from it is when you learn another language. There is a really good reason why most people don't start speaking in a language they are learning – they know that they are going to make a lot of really basic mistakes because they haven't been speaking the language their whole lives. Taking those first steps is all but certainly going to result in many mistakes that will make you sound like a child or a toddler. Yet this is also the best way to learn a language. Most people who speak the language natively are going to be excited to hear it and will be more than happy to help you learn. This is particularly true if you are working with a language partner.

You can use every perceived failure or mistake as a chance to learn. Something went wrong, and it may even be that what happened wasn't necessarily a fault with you or what you did. Maybe you didn't get a job because someone else was more qualified. There is probably some area where you can improve your knowledge base, skills, or experience to be successful the next time. Don't be afraid to ask when you hear you don't get a job, get a bad review, or other event that you perceive as a mistake or failure. Use these as times when you can learn, and then take positive steps to improve. You can also make your daily affirmations work to help establish a positive mindset for the next time.

Harnessing the power of reframing negative perceptions into positive affirmations is akin to turning a darkened room into a space bathed in light. Each affirmation becomes a ray of sunshine, casting out the shadows of negativity and focusing the mind on positive potential. But how does one go about achieving this cognitive transformation? The first step is to identify the negative perceptions. These are often present as self-deprecating thoughts, such as "I'm not good enough", "I always fail", or "I am unworthy." Understand that these thoughts are not inherently true, they are simply manifestations of fear, insecurity, or past disappointment. Having made note of these negative perceptions, the next step is to reframe them. You can reframe a negative thought by focusing on its opposite. If you constantly believe "I'm not good enough", reframe it as "I am enough, just as I am." Persist in this reframing process until the positive affirmation becomes the dominant thought.

Incorporating these transformed thoughts into daily life is paramount. Write them down, read them out loud, or use them as mantras during your daily meditation. Visualize the positive affirmation as a true statement about yourself. Believe in it. Developing gratitude is another important facet of this process. Wake up each day and acknowledge something for which you are grateful. Doing so programs the brain to start recognizing favorable circumstances over unfavorable ones. Acknowledge your small victories too. Each achievement, no matter how minor, is a building block towards greater self-confidence. Recognizing these victories not only boosts happiness levels but also paves the way for the realization of bigger goals. Seek out positive stimulation. Surround yourself with people who inspire and motivate you. Read books that enlighten you and share stories of successful individuals who have overcome the odds. Their journeys can serve as brilliant sources of encouragement. Constant repetition is critical. Our brains have a tendency to revert to familiar patterns. However, with regular reinforcement and by maintaining consistency, new neural pathways can form, enabling your freshly positive mindset to take hold firmly and effectively. The intriguing part is that when you embrace this practice, the world around you starts responding in tune. Individuals start recognizing your renewed confidence and positivity, opening doors to new possibilities. This positive energy then sets off a ripple effect, enhancing not just your own life, but positively impacting those around you.

Remember - transformation is a journey, not a destination. There will be roadblocks. Negative thoughts may resurface, and times may come when self-doubt creeps in. When this happens, recommit to the process. Your persistence and steadfastness will serve as the catalyst for a prosperous life. Reframing negative perceptions into positive affirmations involves recognizing and redefining one's negative thoughts, integrating positive affirmations into daily life, developing gratitude and cherishing small victories, seeking positive stimuli, and practicing consistency and repetition. Overcoming challenges and persisting on this path is the key to unlocking a fulfilling, prosperous life that is not only beneficial to oneself but also has a positive impact on others.

This cognitive transformation is not merely about achieving happiness; it is about thriving and unlocking one's full potential.

Let's look at a practical exercise when it comes to failure:

Adopt The Growth Mindset: Thinking our way to resilience.

Embrace a growth mindset; acknowledge that every failure is a stepping stone towards success. This exercise involves shifting your thought patterns:

1. Identify fixed mindset thoughts - These are thoughts that block your growth, such as „I can't do it" or „It's too difficult".

2. Challenge these thoughts - Ask yourself, „is this really true?" This will encourage you to find ways around the obstacle.

3. Replace the fixed mindset thoughts with growth mindset thoughts - „I can do difficult things" or „Challenges help me to grow".

Nurturing a growth mindset builds your resilience to bounce back from setbacks quickly while seeing the potential growth that can come from failure.

Journal Exercise:

1. Write down a failure or setback that you've recently experienced. Instead of viewing this negatively, identify three valuable lessons this failure has taught you.

2. Think of a time when a setback led to a better outcome in the future. How did that situation make you feel? Write down your feelings and thoughts.

3. Write a personal affirmation that you could use to inspire positivity and resilience during times of failure.
4. How can you apply the lessons you've learned from past failures to current or future situations? Write down two actions you plan on taking.
5. Like learning a new language, day-to-day life presents opportunities for growth from our mistakes. List down three such daily activities where you can apply this mindset.
6. Can you think of a person who demonstrates resilience in the face of failure? What qualities do they have that you admire, and how can you incorporate these qualities into your own life?
7. Reflect on the idea of seeking feedback after setbacks. Who in your life could provide you with constructive criticism and how do you plan on approaching them?

Take a Mental Break

When you are feeling stressed or upset, escape from the situation, physically, if possible, but at least mentally. When you are sitting at work, getting worked up over a particularly bad meeting, exchange, or ridiculous deadline, separate yourself from the situation (going out for a quick walk can be fantastic to help you mentally break from the emotions, but it may not always be possible). Sit back, take a deep breath, and think about some of the things that have gone right up to that point. It doesn't have to be work related – maybe you got a good night's sleep, your kids were easy to get ready for school, or your favorite snack was available in the cafeteria. It's important to keep your mind from focusing solely on the things that are upsetting and to reflect on the things that made you smile, laugh, or feel pleased, even if only for a moment. It will go a long way to making those bad moments a lot more bearable and less mentally draining.

This is definitely more difficult in your personal life because it is ... personal. There isn't really a way to escape it, but you can still look for ways to center yourself and to think about the positives. You may not be able to escape a negative situation in quite the same way, but you definitely have a lot more positives from which to draw in your personal life.

CHAPTER 6

Spreading the Positivity

This is the part that some people dread because it is when you start actually practicing positivity a bit more openly and honestly. It could make you think of those incredibly positive people who can be exhausting to talk to, and that is not the kind of person you want to be. That's not what spreading positivity means, though it could be a good thing to learn to appreciate those people, at least in small doses, because positivity can be incredibly infectious when taken in smaller doses.

Spreading positivity is about helping other people feel the kind of positivity you have been practicing. This doesn't mean interrupting them and interjecting a positive idea since that is one way to make people feel negative emotions. Nor should you try to get them to think of three positives for every negative they discuss. Sometimes people just need to vent, then you can help guide them to a topic that will make them feel positive emotions. Sometimes it's just being there for someone and providing a positive comment or idea when they are having a hard time.

This chapter will give you the simplest actions you can take to spread positivity.

You don't have to be a positive ball of light and energy going around spreading positivity. More often than not, it's the little things that really tend to make a difference and help to make people feel positively about their day. The following suggestions may seem simple, obvious, or too easy, but once you start to use them, you'll find that these five actions can go a long way to seeing positive results in the people around you. The thing to keep in mind is to use the actions in moderation and when appropriate – you'll see what this means as you start to go over them.

Smile a Bit more

Yes, your automatic reaction to seeing that idea is probably to cringe, roll your eyes, or feel a bit offended. This shows how certain actions have tainted a very basic action that can actually help spread positivity without ever having to say a word. The point isn't to feel attractive or to make people more comfortable with your presence – it's to show happiness to let people know how you are feeling.

The smile is one of the most easily recognized facial expressions, so that even toddlers and infants can recognize what it means. When you smile around other adults, there may be an initial reaction of wondering what you've gotten up to – it's also a sign that they are probably parents. Most of them are more likely to smile back because that is just a natural reaction. When you smile without prompting, people tend to register that, and whether or not they know it, they will at least have the corners of their mouth twitch up.

Those who are more aware will probably say something about your smile, with comments like "Someone's in a good mood," and "Looks like you had a good night," being incredibly common responses to seeing someone smile. This goes to show how smiling isn't nearly so common, especially at work. It's also probably why people are more likely to smile in response. Seeing someone who is visibly showing happiness causes most people to feel a sense of empathy and smile in response. Faking a smile isn't always going to make you feel happy, but smiling in response to someone else smiling is much more likely to create at least a fleeting sense of happiness just as a response to the positive image of happiness.

If you want an easy way of spreading positivity without a word, this can be your go-to action. It doesn't cost anything and can help most people around you feel a little bit better.

On the surface, the adage "smile and the world smiles with you," might seem just another feel-good, motivational phrase. But extensive scientific research exists that supports and bolsters this old saying, extending its relevance from mere rhetoric to an advantageous action with both psychological and physiological benefits. One area that the scientific community has deeply explored is the connection between smiling and our brain. Several psychological studies reveal that smiling, even an artificial one, can stimulate the brain as much as receiving a substantial monetary reward. In fact, each time a smile flashes across your face, your brain does a little party dance, releasing a cocktail of neurotransmitters – dopamine, endorphins, and serotonin. These biochemical agents together act as natural antidepressants, alleviating stress and generating feelings of overall happiness and contentment. In a 2010 research conducted by Hewlett and Watson, it was found that smiling activates the release of neuropeptides that work toward fighting off stress. Additionally, simple muscular changes caused by smiling can trick the brain into perceiving happiness, thus improving the mood. This phenomenon, termed 'Facial-Feedback Hypothesis,' suggests how our brain reacts to stimuli that engender emotion and that the mere act of smiling can create a reciprocal improve mood.

Another dimension to this 'smile science' pertains to our physical health. When the brain feels happy, it instructs the body to relax and be more energetic, indirectly boosting the immune system. In simple terms, smiling can be your secret weapon against diseases, increasing longevity as well as improving overall quality of life. It even lowers your heart rate, provides better pain management, and significantly reduces blood pressure. The 'world' in the adage isn't metaphorical either. Smiles are like ripples, influencing the 'smile environment.' They induce 'mirror neurons' located in the frontal cortex of people you interact with, thereby promoting a reciprocal smile. So, when you smile, you are indirectly creating a positive atmosphere, fostering conviviality. Studies show that people intuitively trust those who smile often. They are perceived as more friendly, approachable, and trustworthy, giving them an edge, especially in social scenarios and professional circles. Not only does this foster supportive relationships, but it can fire up a spiraling wave of positivity. In essence, when you smile, you are not just inviting happiness into your life but also spreading joy in the world around you.

While the powerful impacts of the simple act of smiling may seem outlandishly exaggerated, the scientific backing pushes the efficacy of the 'smile to feel good' theory from just an assumption to a reality. Like Newton's Third Law of Motion, for every action, there is an equal and opposite reaction. So, it turns out that the action of flashing a wide, healthy smile not only does wonders for your brain and body but can also brighten up the world around you, injecting more positivity into the system, thus proving the adage true in all respects.

In order to incorporate more genuine smiles into your daily routines, there are several exercises that you could practice. The main goal of these practices is to allow expressions of joy to flow naturally, mitigating any forced effort. The by-product is authenticity, which significantly augments positive responses from people around you.

To start, devote a few minutes each day to reflect on happy moments.

Remember, to genuinely smile, one needs to draw from genuine sources of happiness. Take time from your schedule to reminisce positive memories, be it a splendid vacation, a good joke, or a cherished memory with a loved one. As your mind wanders these pleasant memories, allow your smile to organically follow your thoughts.

Another technique is mindful smiling. This is an exercise that involves smiling for no particular reason. It may feel awkward initially, but with practice, it will foster a more natural expression of happiness. Sit in a quiet space. Close your eyes and relax your face muscles. Gradually, form a subtle smile, dwelling on the positive feelings it brings.

Try "mirror practice". Stand in front of a mirror and practice different kinds of smiles. Observe and analyze which ones seem forced and which ones radiate genuine warmth. Keep practicing till your centered, natural smile becomes a part of your muscle memory.

And lastly, make smiling a part of your routine activities. Whether you are reading, cooking, walking, or working on your computer, remind yourself to smile. It's interesting how soon these little reminders transform into a habit, providing you with a happier disposition, irrespective of the activity involved.

Concerning authenticity, it is that unspoken element that makes a smile contagious. Authenticity in a smile signals honesty and openness to the human brain. When a smile is genuine, it indicates that the person is genuinely pleasant and approachable, leading to a positive response from others. If the smile is inauthentic or forced, it may unnerve or repel people, making social interactions less productive or detrimental. Authentic smiles generate a cyclical effect where the positivity radiated through the authentic expression is reciprocated by the people around you. As a result, you tend to feel more content, bringing more authenticity to your smiles, henceforth enhancing your interpersonal relationships and overall well-being. Authenticity in a smile leads to more positive thoughts and actions. Research has shown that managing to crack a genuine smile even on tough days can uplift mood and create a snowball effect of positivity. People are more likely to respond favorably to genuine emotions, which in turn increases the likelihood of you having more reasons to smile! Incorporating authentic smiles in your day-to-day life is both an art and a skill. Practice these exercises every day, and soon you will notice a shift in your mindset, attitude, and more importantly, the quality of your interactions and relationships, all thanks to the power of authentic smiling.

Journal Exercise:

1. Reflect on a moment when someone's genuine smile made you feel happy. How did it affect your mood?
2. Try to recall a time in your professional environment where smiling was considered an unusual or even inappropriate behavior. Reflect on what impact the lack of smiles might have had on interpersonal relationships and overall professionalism.
3. Think about your own smiling habits. How often do you smile sincerely during your everyday activities? Do you notice others reciprocating your own genuine smiles?
4. Recall a situation when someone else's joy prompted empathetic reactions in you. How did that incident affect your overall mood or behavior?
5. Finally, envision how you can be more proactive about smiling truly in the future. Reflect on situations where your smile could be a powerful tool to spread positivity.
6. Have you ever noticed a difference in feeling between faking a smile and reciprocating a genuine one? Elaborate on your thoughts.

Remember, this exercise is not about forcing or faking positivity, but about becoming conscious of the power of your genuine joy and the impact it can have on others as well as yourself.

Help When You Can

They say that it doesn't cost anything to be nice, well, this is just an extension of that. When you see someone who could use a bit of help, step in. This can simply be holding the door when someone has their arms full, stopping and helping someone who is hanging a shop outside their shop, or helping someone carry stuff when their arms are overloaded.

You do need to be careful. Don't approach strangers to help them put their stuff in their car or in their own yard (unless they are neighbors) because this does come off as a bit creepy. When you help people, do it out in public where other people can see so that you don't make them uncomfortable.

Of course, you should help people you know well, especially loved ones. Make it clear that you are there to help them. You can also offer an ear to someone who seems upset or distressed. Practice using empathy when you are in public, and that will spread positivity around that will have longer lasting effects.

Empathetic positive action in public settings is a roadmap to spreading positivity, cultivating understanding, and ensuring a more inclusive space for everyone. It's about harnessing empathetic feelings and connecting with others on a personal level - seeing things from a different perspective and taking actions that reflect this understanding.

Embracing empathy is as much about individual transformation as it is about communal. It's about self-growth and fostering a society where understanding and acceptance are the norms. By taking the time to exercise empathy in public settings, you not only offer a beacon of support to those in need, but you also strengthen your capacity for compassion and kindness, which is the bedrock of our shared humanity. Remember, every empathetic action, no matter how small, can make a significant difference in someone's life and gradually, the world at large. Without question, understanding the necessity of transparency and tact in providing help is essential; what's more crucial is figuring out how to do so while keeping other people's comfort in view—a rewarding but sometimes challenging task.

Let's consider acquaintances. Moving beyond the rims of casual conversations to the area of caring support can be delicate. Primarily, be patient, because rapid moves may create discomfort. It's essential not to assume that your help is required, allow them to take the lead — this is the crux of tact in these situations. Transparent communication is crucial here; express your willingness to provide support but do not force it upon them. Use open-ended questions to encourage dialogue, and show empathy, not sympathy.

Now, on to loved ones. Here, the stakes tend to be higher. Effective, supportive communication with loved ones is much about timing, tone, and emotional competency. Be sensitive with words and remember, often, silence can be golden too. Be aware of non-verbal communication – comforting silence, a reassuring pat on the back or a warm hug can genuinely demonstrate your empathy. Your attention, patience, and understanding go a far way in showing your support. However, keep in mind that our loved ones may not always turn to us for help. Your role isn't to "fix" everything but to offer a secure, non-judgmental space where they can be vulnerable.

Engaging with strangers in a moment of need is different ball game altogether. Empathy, coupled with respect for boundaries, is the key here. Understanding that we all have our unique methods of addressing our challenges, and figuring out where you fit in the puzzle, can dictate the level of support you provide. Show respect for their choices and decision-making abilities; refrain from advice bombardment. Being transparent about your intentions and avoidance of any ulterior motives is vital; doing otherwise will compromise trust.

In all these situations, it's important to understand that it's not about you, but about them. Your role should be akin to a lighthouse, guiding ships safely to shore, not a tugboat dragging them in. Here, knowledge and wisdom are paramount. Remember, it's possible to say the right thing in a wrong way.

Also, remember there may be times when professional help may be necessary. It can be difficult to step back, but understand it's okay not to have all the answers. Offering to connect them to professional resources can be a great sign of real support.

In summary:

- ➲ Understand the persona and comfort level of the person in need.
- ➲ Exercise patience. Allow them to guide the pace.
- ➲ Be transparent about your intentions and maintain a no-strings-attached attitude.
- ➲ Use open-ended questions to spark dialogue with acquaintances and loved ones.
- ➲ Be aware of body language and non-verbal cues; they hold significant weight.
- ➲ Respect the decision-making abilities of those you aim to help.
- ➲ Avoid the „fix-it“ attitude; provide a secure, non-judgmental space instead.
- ➲ Be prepared to step back when professional help is required.

Remember, there is power in vulnerability, and by exercising transparency and tact, we can create a comforting environment that nurtures trust, empathy, and genuine help.

Journal Exercise:

1. Journal about a time when you performed a random act of kindness. How did it make you feel and what was the other person's response?
2. Reflect on a situation where someone helped you when you least expected it. What impact did it have on you? How can you pay it forward?

3. Remember a moment where you wanted to help someone but didn't feel comfortable. In hindsight, what could you have done differently?
4. Imagine yourself in a public setting. How could you demonstrate empathy and spread positivity to strangers without making them feel uncomfortable?
5. How can you communicate better with your loved ones or close acquaintances about your intentions to help without invasive?
6. Think of a personal action plan to incorporate kindness into your daily routine. How will this contribute to creating a mutually respectful and positive environment?

Even small actions can have significant ripple effects. Reflect on these scenarios and remember them the next time you head out the door!

Be Less Negative When Speaking or Acting

Everyone needs to vent from time to time, but don't make venting and complaining a part of your regular interaction with anyone. When you are feeling upset, annoyed, or bothered, find a way to get it out of your system without spreading a lot of negativity around you. Exercising or being active is one of the best ways to manage negative emotions, but you may have something else that helps you mitigate a bad mood. There doesn't have to be a reason for being in a bad mood – everyone wakes up on the wrong side of the bed from time to time. Just don't let that mean that you take your bad mood out on others. Find productive ways to address and manage your mood. Definitely avoid spreading it around you.

This doesn't mean that you shouldn't seek help or talk to people about problems. You want to be there for the people you care about, and they want to be there for you. Just don't make most of your conversations negative. If you are having a rough time, you can seek help from a professional to help you through particularly rough periods. Use your support group, but don't rely on them to overcome issues when you should be talking to someone who can give you an objective perspective.

Have you ever considered the true power of words? It's remarkable how our everyday conversations, interlaced with certain words, subtly impact our emotional and mental state. Words carry energy; they are powerful, affecting our emotions directly. Often, the impact of negative language permeates our psyche stealthily.

1. We cannot deny the fact that we live in a society where a sea of words engulfs our senses. As individuals, we tend to absorb these words, often unconsciously. Studies indicate that negative words — those inherently associated with harmful emotions — can influence our brain function, causing stress or leading us into a cycle of negative thinking.

2. Prolonged exposure to negative conversations can be subtly harmful. Projecting a harsh view of the world, they bombard the mind with the distressing imagery which could accumulate over time to become chronic stressors. Over time, these stressors can alter the brain's structure, leading to an increased likelihood of developing mood disorders or behavioral issues.

3. Now that we've understood the potential harm caused by negative words, let's venture into the realm of positivity. Adopting a positive verbal communication style has immense benefits, and here are some guidelines to aid you on this journey.

   i. Be Mindful: Pay attention to the words used in your conversation. Are they generally positive or negative? Monitor your speech and actively control the words you use.

   ii. Word Replacement: Substitute negative words for positive ones. For instance, instead of using 'I can't', use 'I'll find a way'.

iii. Practice Gratitude: Expressing gratitude on a daily basis can significantly infuse positivity into your life and language.

iv. Look for the Silver Lining: Even in difficult situations, try to find a positive takeaway. This practice alone can transform your verbal communication.

Making these guidelines a part of your daily routine can be life-changing. Over time, they will assist in turning your attention towards more positive, healthy conversations, eventually making them a part of your natural thinking process. Remember, words carry energy, and the words you use determine the type of energy you both give and receive. Make it positive.

Journal Exercise:

1. Reflect on a recent situation where you may have allowed negativity to take over your mood and in turn your conversations. Detail the circumstance, and describe how your behavior may have impacted those around you.

2. List three physical activities or personal interests that make you happy or serve as a positive outlet for you. How can these help you manage your negative emotions?

3. Recall a time when you shared your concerns with a loved one versus engaging in a negative conversation. What were the differences in those two interactions, and how did they make you feel?

4. Think about the support system you have in place for when times get challenging. Can you name a time that seeking professional guidance could have provided more constructive solutions than relying only on your support system?

5. Based on reflections from this exercise, create three strategies you aim to adopt in your day-to-day life to be less negative when speaking or acting.

Spread Positivity on Social Media

There is a good reason why social media gets a lot of flak – it is one of the easiest ways to spread negativity, and people tend to do that very freely. The anonymity of being behind a keyboard helps people feel comfortable saying and doing things that inspire negative emotions.

You can be a great counter to this, offering positivity to people online. Since you can reach a much wider audience, this can help spread positivity around much faster than you can in person. Make an effort to post a positive message every day, or if you are having a particularly good day, post a couple of positive messages to let people know you are feeling great.

Share good news, funny videos, and other things that inspire positive emotions to help people feel positive emotions for at least a little while. Spend time giving positive reactions to your family and friends, dropping a happy or supportive comment. Share a positive story about something that happened to you that day – this will also help you to focus on the positives as well. Snap a picture of your pets to make people feel a bit warm and fuzzy – there isn't anything quite so popular as cats and dogs being cute, goofy, or mischievous. Over time, people will probably enjoy viewing what you have to say and do, even if they don't let you know that they appreciate it. Finding people on social media who spread positivity is like finding an oasis in the desert – it's rare and people will come back to it as often as they can to get a boost of positivity in their day.

Take some time to look for other positive people on social media to help you too. You need to have a bit of positivity to help inspire you to keep in a positive mindset, especially when you venture onto social media sites.

Here are a few ways and techniques to help you create and maintain a consistent stream of positive posts:

1. Develop a content calendar: Scheduling your posts can ensure you stick to a positive theme. It will also help align your content with upcoming holidays and events, so you connect with your audience on what is top of their mind.

2. Start your day with a positivity kickoff: A quick, uplifting message to kickstart your followers' day can set the mood and build trust in your consistency.

3. Transparent Communication: Viewers appreciate honesty. In case of events that could impact your output (such as personal emergencies), communicating these—or at least, letting your followers know there might be changes—helps maintain respect between you and your audience.

Dealing with backlash or negative responses is another crucial aspect of internet engagement. Here are strategies to handle these situations effectively:

1. Respond, not react: When confronted with negative comments, it is vital to respond thoughtfully rather than reacting impulsively. A calm and composed response reflects maturity and positivity.

2. Learn from criticism: Not all negative responses are necessarily harmful. Constructive criticism can provide useful insight into areas needing improvement.

3. Apologize when necessary: If an error has occurred, an apology can resolve the issue and restore your audience's faith.

4. Ignore or block trolls: Distinguish between genuine comments and trolls seeking attention. Eliminating negativity from trolls helps maintain a positive social space.

By continuously refining and enhancing these strategies, you can become a beacon of positivity on social media. Regardless of the challenges or setbacks you face, remember that every situation offers an opportunity to learn, grow and to become better at what we do. Stay resilient, and very soon, your digital sphere will radiate with positivity and optimism.

Embracing the world of social media is akin to diving into a vast, vibrant ocean. As such, it's crucial to make this space, an oasis of optimism. The secret lies in finding, connecting, and engaging with positivity-oriented users.

Start by conducting research to find positivity-oriented users. A good start is looking for hashtags related to positivity, optimism, motivation, or whatever field you're interested in. On Instagram, positivity packed hashtags such as #Positivity or #SpreadLove abound. On Twitter, explore tags like #MondayMotivation or #Inspire to boost your feed. Once you have these targets, browse through, and start following and interacting with these individuals.

You can comment on their posts and even send direct messages to express your appreciation or share your thoughts. Mentioning how their posts have uplifted you or helped maintain your positivity can spark a meaningful connection. Remember, genuine interactions create a more durable bond.

At the same time, be conscious of your own posts too. Reflect positivity, share motivational quotes, uplifting content, or inspiring stories. Your content will magnetize similar-minded users who can contribute to your online oasis of optimism. Regularity ensures visibility and keeps your message at the forefront of your followers' minds.

A crucial aspect to stay connected and develop deeper relationships is participation. Join positivity-centered groups on platforms like Facebook or LinkedIn. Participate in discussions, share insightful content, lend support to those who seek it and foster a give-and-take relationship. This interaction will nurture your network, making them reliable resources for overcoming negativity. To maintain engagement with your network, consistent communication is essential. Wish your followers good mornings or share an inspiring quote in the evening; conduct live video sessions or create weekly challenges circling positivity. These activities will keep your community engaged and encourage interaction. Additionally, utilize the gift of collaboration. Often, social media users host joint lives, challenges or webinars. Reach out to these positivity-oriented users for such collaborations. This practice not only strengthens your bond with them but also exposes you to their followers, expanding your optimistic network. Preparing a calendar for regular collaborations will ensure ongoing interaction.

Your positive oasis is as much about giving as receiving. Take the time to support those in your community. If someone shares an achievement, congratulate them. If they share a struggle, offer words of encouragement. The community you build would act as a shield against negativity, a sanctuary for hope, happiness, and inspiration. Furthermore, these connections can act as a constant source of mutual support, a network of cheerleaders helping lift each other's spirits. Such uplifting engagement nurtures a sense of belonging, validating experiences and propelling further positivity. By diving into specific methods of finding, connecting, and engaging with other positivity-oriented users on social media, you can effectively build an online oasis of optimism. This doesn't just foster a positive influence on your daily life but also turns social media into a cheerful companion radiating positivity, hope, and inspiration in every scroll.

Journal Exercise:

1. Reflect on your current social media usage and describe the type of content you tend to share most often.

2. Consider situations in the past week where you could have shared a positive experience but didn't. Why did you decide not to share it?

3. Identify three specific actions you can take to start spreading positivity on your social media platforms.

4. Imagine the impact of your positive posts. How do you think they would affect your audience's mood and perspective?
5. Think about the people you interact with on social media. Which of them can serve as your allies in promoting positivity? Why did you choose them?
6. How will you ensure that you maintain this positive approach on social media amidst the negativity you might encounter online?
7. Finally, write a commitment statement to yourself emphasizing your decision to spread positivity online and describe why it's important to you.

Be Free with Compliments

Being complimentary toward other people is an easy way to spread positivity. At work, let someone know that something they did really helped you or that they did a great job on something you reviewed. In your personal life, talk about stories that highlight tasks that they do well. Even in public, if you see someone with an outfit you love, let them know.

Do be careful about compliments that focus solely on appearance. You want to focus on the person, not the appearance. Positive comments about outfits are safe because it is something that the person chose to wear, showing off their fashion sense. Praising a hairstyle is something else that can let people know you think they did a fantastic job because it takes skill to do a lot of hairstyles. Avoid telling people they look like models or that they look hot. These kinds of compliments come off as being creepy, and people don't really have much control over their baseline appearance – that's genetics. Make compliments that a person can take as a positive about themselves, not about genetic luck.

You don't need to go overboard, but working to give one compliment a day can really help to put you in a more positive frame of mind as you need to be more mindful of the world around you to issue a compliment. You don't have to walk into your office, school, or home and start offering compliments to everyone, unless you are in a really good mood and want to help everyone else feel the same way. Just take the time to really appreciate the people around you and let them know that you appreciate them through compliments. It's an incredibly easy thing you can do that can help others experience some positivity too.

The power of praise - the mere words seemingly floating in the ether between two individuals - carries both unseen weight and potential. It's a combination of chemical reactions, societal conditioning, and emotional response that renders praise a potent tool in influencing behavior, enhancing relationships, and fostering positivity. Let's look at the biochemistry of the brain. How does it react when we receive praise, and why does that matter significantly? The neurotransmitters serotonin, dopamine, and oxytocin are critical players in this scenario. Here's how they work:

1. Serotonin, also known as the ‚happy chemical,' surges when we are complimented, eliciting feelings of contentment and happiness. Higher levels of serotonin contribute to the overall wellbeing and positivity, providing an emotional boost that encourages the recipient to repeat the behavior that led to the accolade.

2. Dopamine, often linked to the brain's reward system, is another significant character in this play. When we receive praise, this neurotransmitter takes the stage, giving us that sense of accomplishment and pleasure. The brain enjoys this „reward" and thus, enforces the behavior that led to the affirmation.

3. Oxytocin, though typically associated with social bonding and trust, also plays a role within this context. Compliments from a trusted person increase oxytocin levels, implying that interpersonal relationships can

be strengthened through the simple act of expressing genuine praise.

Just as our brains have a biochemical response to praise, our psychosocial reactions should not be overlooked either. Praising a child's effort, for instance, fuels their motivation and instills an enhanced sense of ability. Encouraging a coworker can significantly improve their job satisfaction and productivity, cultivating a work environment that fosters mutual respect and cooperation.

We, humans, are social creatures. We crave validation and acceptance from our peers. When we receive praise, it confirms that we are valued and that our actions are positively affecting others, providing a powerful source of motivation to continue those behaviors. The psychology and science behind praise offer us profound insights into its power and potential in building relationships, nurturing positivity, and contributing to personal growth. Next time one extends a compliment, perhaps a moment's pause could be taken to appreciate the rich psychological processes it may initiate. In doing so, praise may be recognized not only as a tool for affirmation but also as a bridge to meaningful human connection. The art of complimenting is not inherent, it is acquired, harness-able and can be significantly improved through practice. Here are a few practical exercises for you to engage in, to help you better your skills:

1. The Mirror Exercise: Set aside time each day to identify three things you genuinely like about yourself. These can be physical attributes or personality traits. This exercise not only boosts your self-esteem and self-awareness but it also helps you better recognize positive attributes in others, hence making your compliments sincere and meaningful.

2. Visualizing Positivity: Close your eyes and visualize a person. Think about the positive qualities they possess. Visualizing their strengths can help you internalize the kind words you say about them, making your compliments more authentic.

3. Practicing Timing: Compliments should not feel rushed or out of place. They should be relevant and well timed. A good exercise for this is to compliment someone during a conversation only when it flows naturally, without forcing or awkwardly inserting a compliment.

4. Uplifting Support: Use compliments as a tool to uplift someone going through a challenging situation. This shows compassion and sensitivity, and enhances your ability to give sincere and appropriate compliments.

5. Constructive Compliments: Gear your compliments towards skills and abilities that the person is trying to improve. This promotes positivity and shows that you are supportive, and your compliments are thought out and not aimless praise.

6. Setting Compliment Goals: Set a goal to give a certain number of compliments per day. Remember, the purpose is not to meet a quota but to foster a more positive, appreciative outlook towards others.

Remember, the delivery of the compliment matters as much as its content. For example, making eye contact and saying the compliment with a warm and friendly tone can make a significant difference. Being conscious of your non-verbal communication ensures that the compliment is received as intended.

Journal Exercise:

1. Reflect on a time you offered a genuine and sincere compliment to someone. How did you feel before and after giving the compliment? How did the recipient react?

2. Think of a compliment you have received in the past that truly made your day. What was it about that compliment that made it so meaningful to you?

3. Now, based on what you have learnt from this chapter, what could be some of the qualities or actions you can start recognizing and complimenting in others?

4. Can you think of one person you could offer a sincere compliment to tomorrow? Write down who it is, and why you think they deserve a compliment. Practice the compliment in a way that it makes them feel seen and valued but also comfortable.

5. Reflect on the impact of this positivity practice on your mindset if you were to persistently give at least one genuine compliment a day. How do you think this could affect your day-to-day outlook?

CHAPTER 7

Practicing Gratitude to Improve Positive Thinking

Practicing gratitude is something that most people fail to do, not because they aren't grateful for what they have, but because it doesn't seem necessary. After all, as long as you say thank you when someone gives you something, what else is there, right?

Gratitude goes beyond just having good manners though. It is a habit that happier people tend to practice all of the time. When you stop and take the time to be appreciative of what you have, it helps inspire positive emotions in yourself, not just when you thank someone for helping or giving you a gift. It's also nice to be thanked because it means that someone is recognizing your efforts, thoughtfulness, or something you've done. However, you should also practice gratitude on your own because a lot of things that you are thankful for are either a result of your hard work or good fortune. For example, there is nobody to specifically thank when you reach a personal goal. Unless you have a trainer, coach, instructor, or teacher helping you through an activity, the gratitude you are expressing is really to yourself for sticking it out and achieving your goal. Of course, you should thank people for helping you get to your goal, but you should also think about the things that you are grateful for having in your own time. You put the effort into it, so be thankful that you did, as well as allowing yourself time to reflect on the fact that you are grateful for the things you have, whether they are a product of your own work or because you have been fortunate in life.

This chapter covers some suggestions of very basic things you can do to practice gratitude, with a number of them combining with elements of being mindful since that is the best way to become more aware of what you actually have. Once we acquire or achieve something, we often tend to start taking it for granted almost immediately and set our eyes on the next goal. Practicing gratitude is one way to remind yourself of the things that make our lives enjoyable by making sure we don't take them for granted. You don't have to practice all of these ideas. Unlike a lot of the other activities covered in this book, gratitude is a feeling that people tend to have preferences about, and those preferences aren't going to change much over time. The point is to keep practicing gratitude over your life to help you be mindful of the things that make your life better.

Be Observant

Most of us are in the habit of saying thank you. It's great and shows good manners, but it also means that you aren't really thinking about the way you feel – it is an automatic reaction, not a sincere expression of gratitude. Start paying attention to when you say thank you and work to actually mean it on a level that is more self-aware. When you are more aware of the times you are expressing thanks, you will actually have a stronger emotional response to it, and that is almost always going to be a positive emotional response.

You can also be more observant of things in your life that you are thankful for that don't require you to verbally express that gratitude. As you know when you get older, you are much more grateful for feeling good in the morning. After you've been sick, you are more aware of feeling healthy for at least a few days. Try to stretch this gratitude out over a longer period of time. If you have a new video game, book, or recipe that you want to try, take a moment to feel grateful for it because all of these things inspire a sense of excitement and positivity in your life. And don't forget to be grateful for the good relationships that you have with family members and friends! Where would you be without them?

We are surrounded by things that make our lives better, but we stop noticing them after a while. Take the time to observe your surroundings and your life for the things that you know you are fortunate to have and reflect on how those things improve your life.

Improving observational skills is not a process that happens overnight. It's an exercise that requires concerted effort and active engagement with your surroundings. From actively noticing the warmth of the sun on your skin, to acknowledging the efforts of a loved one preparing a meal, everything can be an object of our attention. Once we have trained ourselves to observe more attentively, we begin to notice the smaller details that often go unnoticed, these observations serve as the basis for cultivating deeper gratitude.

Practicing gratitude can be consciously practiced. To help you in the beginning, you can use three types of observations for practicing gratitude. These help as a guideline, later, when you've become more proficient, you won't need to practice these consciously anymore:

1. Visual observation: Challenge yourself to take in the detailed elements of your surroundings. Notice the texture of a leaf, the way light filters through your window, or the non-verbal cues displayed by your partner or friends. These visual cues often hide a multitude of blessings we unwittingly take for granted.

2. Auditory observations: There is music in everyday sounds, be it the rustle of the trees, the chirping of birds, or the hum of a busy street. Paying attention to these sounds, noticing their ebb and flow, and their connection to the world around us, can foster a profound appreciation for the world we live in.

3. Empathic observation: Understanding the labor or thought that someone put into an action for you

encourages a significant sense of gratitude. By empathetically acknowledging their work, you identify and appreciate their effort, fostering a genuine sense of thanks.

Journal Exercise:

1. Write down five things from your day today that you are grateful for. As you write each item, try to remember the specific moment you felt gratitude and describe it in detail.
2. Reflect on your pattern of saying „thank you". Do you find it has become more of an automatic response? If yes, write down three instances where it was more automatic than genuine, and propose how you can transform this into a heartfelt gratitude next time.
3. Identify two positive things in your environment that you usually overlook and write why you're grateful for them.
4. Do you think being observant has affected your ability to appreciate life's blessings? Write down your feelings about this and examples in support of your answer.
5. Summarize this chapter in your own words. Reflect on how its principles could be implemented in your life to enhance your well-being and happiness.

Start or End Your Day by Being Thankful for Three Things

This exercise is one that most people know about, but it also seems a bit silly. For a lot of people (especially children and teenagers), the three things they mention are more jokes than serious. Even that is fine because they are still thinking about what they are thankful for in their lives. It is also something you can do as a family, though you should probably practice thinking of three things on your own before practicing with others.

Actually, you should say or write out what you are grateful for instead of just thinking of them in passing. You need to actually sit and really think about what you are grateful for so that you are more aware and mindful. Try to come up with new things to be thankful for each day because this shouldn't be an exercise in repetition, but in being aware of what you have that improves your life. As you get accustomed to doing this, you can start practicing gratitude with your family. Even if they are annoyed by it, when kids get older, they are more likely to be aware of the things that they have that make them happy. They may be too immature to fully appreciate the things they have as kids and teens, but practicing when they are young will help most of them to be more aware as they age. Someday they may even thank you for helping them express gratitude and be more aware, and practicing it even if they were brats about it.

It Can Always Be Worse ...

We may think about the worst-case scenarios, but we usually tend to think about how things could be better than they are right now. Sure, things could always be better – but they could also be a lot worse. Things can always be worse. Think about a stressful period in your life or about a time when you were very unhappy, and that will help you find things about your life today that you are grateful for in this part of your life. It's not about negativity, but about remembering that things are different than the last time you were in a rough situation. You have more experience, more understanding, or more support so that you don't have to solve problems on your own. Even if life is rough now, you have things you didn't have before that can help.

Often, when life throws curveballs at us, it's easy to get bogged down by the immediate challenges and lose sight of the broader perspective. That's where the mantra "It can always be worse" comes into play. It's not just a catchphrase to numb our pain but a potent tool to foster gratitude.

The Scale of Life's Challenges: All of us face setbacks, disappointments, and obstacles. Yet, when they occur, it's not unusual to feel as if the weight of the world is resting squarely on our shoulders. However, when we stop and think about the vastness of human experience, we realize our current situation, no matter how dire, is just a small blip in the grand scheme of things. Many before us have faced similar or even more challenging situations and have emerged stronger. Taking a moment to gain this perspective can provide a sense of solace and gratitude for the strength and resilience we possess.

A Gateway to Empathy: By recognizing that our situation could be more challenging, we open the doors to empathy. We become more attuned to the struggles of others and appreciate the blessings we have. Empathy, in turn, enriches our own lives by deepening our connections to others and enhancing our understanding of the world.

Celebrating Small Victories: The realization that things could be worse also allows us to celebrate our small victories. Did you manage to get out of bed and face the day even though you felt defeated? That's a win. Did you make someone smile despite your own turmoil? Another win. These small moments, when viewed through the lens of gratitude, become significant milestones on our journey of positive thinking.

Reflecting on Past Challenges: By remembering a time when things were even harder, we can appreciate how far we've come. This retrospective view offers us tangible proof of our growth, resilience, and ability to overcome. Even if we're facing new challenges today, we can find gratitude in the knowledge that we've faced adversity before and triumphed. This realization not only fosters a sense of gratitude for our journey but also instills confidence in our ability to handle future challenges.

Evolving Our Mindset: Maintaining the perspective that "It can always be worse" isn't about downplaying our current struggles but about evolving our mindset. It's about shifting from a place of lack to one of abundance. By consistently reminding ourselves of this perspective, we train our brain to find silver linings, to appreciate the small blessings, and to always search for reasons to be grateful, no matter the circumstances.

The idea that "It can always be worse" is more than just a coping mechanism; it's a catalyst for fostering genuine gratitude. When we adopt this mindset, we not only improve our mental well-being but also enrich our lives in countless ways. By grounding ourselves in gratitude, we pave the way for lasting positivity, resilience, and joy. So, the next time you're faced with adversity, remember this perspective, embrace the lessons it brings, and let gratitude light your way.

Journal about Your Experiences

Periodically, you can go back through your journal, and that will remind you of what you have acquired since you started writing about your days. Make a point of writing about things that you got that day or things that you are grateful for having as a way of reminding yourself of what you have now.

Gratitude journaling may often give an impression of being a trendy fad, popularized by self-improvement gurus and wellness influencers. Yet, its roots stretch much farther back, and its impact on mental health is backed by substantial psychological research. Simply put, gratitude journaling is the practice of recording and consciously acknowledging what one is grateful for in their lives. Psychologically, gratitude journaling plays a vital role in enhancing our ability to adapt to various life circumstances. It helps in reining in our capacity to focus on negativity by drawing our attention to positivity. Significant psychological studies have indicated that gratitude journaling can boost happiness and reduce depressive symptoms. With consistent practice, it aids in combating mental health issues like stress, anxiety, and depression by creating harmonious emotions. The exploration of the role of gratitude journaling in shaping perspective can be equated with developing a colorful lens through which we can view the world. Shaping a perspective that is rooted in gratefulness allows one to see the silver lining, even in the darkest clouds. By acknowledging and appreciating the blessings, one's disposition towards life noticeably improves, driving a greater sense of fulfillment and optimism.

Gratitude journaling escalates the ability to remain positive in any situation. Essentially, what gratitude journaling does is that it inculcates a habit that casts a ripple effect of positivity in one's thoughts and actions. When family, work, health or any other life precinct tends to sway the emotional equilibrium, gratitude journaling becomes a beacon of hope and positivity. It enables individuals to avoid destructive emotions and bounce back from adversity. Developing this habit helps to create a fortress of positivity that protects us during difficult times.

Implementing gratitude journaling into your routine could include the following steps:

1. Start by choosing a specified time daily to write in your journal. It could be early morning upon waking or just before sleeping.

2. Be genuine with your entries. It doesn't matter how small or big those instances are as long as they have made you feel grateful.

3. Write down even the challenges you faced that day and try recognizing the good in those situations, even if it's just a lesson learned.

4. Pair your journaling with a daily routine, like having your morning coffee or just before you turn off the bedside lamp.

5. Constantly remind yourself why you are doing this. The key to consistent gratitude journaling is staying motivated and understanding the benefits.

Journal Exercise:

1. List down three challenging situations you have faced in the past and for each situation write about how you overcame it and what lessons you learned.
2. Identify three positive things or resources you now possess because of the past challenges, and express gratitude for them.
3. Write about a difficult situation you are currently facing or faced recently and think about how it could actually be worse. Reflect on how you are stronger dealing with this because of your past experiences.
4. Finally, imagine it is one year from now. Write a letter to yourself expressing gratitude for all the growth and learnings that you will encounter in the year. Express optimism and trust in your future self's ability to handle the upcoming situations. Reflect on how hurdles can serve as stepping stones for development.

Get Creative

The way you express your gratitude is incredibly personal. No one can tell you that there is one right way to express your gratitude. If you don't think that any of the suggestions in this chapter will work for you, focus on things that you are grateful for having while you are exercising, meditating, or being mindful. The point is to pay attention to what makes you feel happy or positive about your life. Only you know the best way to tap into being more aware of those things – what's important is to learn to be more actively grateful for all of the good things you have in your life.

Approaching gratitude unconventionally can often yield unexpected and powerful results. Imagine a long day at work, filled with challenges and stresses. You come home, tired and weary. You could collapse on the couch, zoning out with mindless TV, or you could choose a different path - opting for what might initially seem like more work but ends up fulfilling you in surprising ways. Many of these unconventional methods revolve around activities we may already find therapeutic or mind-clearing, like cooking, dancing, or crafting. All these activities allow us to step away from the noise of our lives and fully focus on something else. This is precisely where we find an opportunity to express gratitude.

Take cooking, for example. After a day of work, instead of seeing this as another chore on a long list of to-dos, flip the script and think of it as an opportunity to nourish your body and those you love. Each ingredient you chop, stir, and cook is a chance to honor the earth that produced it. With each bite, appreciate the nutrition and energy it provides. This mindful practice transforms a mundane activity into a moment of profound gratitude for nature's bounty and your body's resilience.

Dancing is another powerful, albeit unexpected, conduit for gratitude. How many times have we caught ourselves swaying to a catchy tune, a beat that resonates within us, or a melody that transports us to another time and place? This mindful movement allows us to connect with our bodies in beautiful ways. Engaging in dance, even if only for a few minutes a day, can be a moment to appreciate the music, the space, and most importantly, the incredible vessel that is your body.

Crafting too can be a novel way to express appreciation. Whether you find solace in knitting, painting, woodworking, or any other form of crafting, each creation provides an opportunity for gratitude. With every stitch, brushstroke, or carved line, appreciate the skill in your hands, the creativity in your mind, and the peace this process brings.

These are just a few examples. The goal is to interrupt the routine, inject mindfulness into regular activities, and find unique ways to express appreciation. Gratitude needn't be confined just to moments of peace and introspection, tucked away in a corner of our busy schedules. It should spill over the boundaries we've built around it, coloring every conversation, every household chore, every creative pursuit, and the most ordinary tasks with deep respect and mindful acknowledgment. Unconventional gratitude practices are much more than fun diversions or interesting ways to keep our minds busy. They offer the potential to connect more deeply with our daily activities. The more we bring mindfulness and intentionality into these practices, the richer and more fulfilling they become, leading not just to a sense of balance but a real profound, often unexplored, appreciation for life.

Journal Exercise:

Take a moment to ponder on the following questions and jot down your thoughts:

1. List three things or people you're most grateful for at this moment. What makes each so special?
2. Is there a particular creative outlet mentioned in this chapter that intrigues you? If so, explain why you find it appealing.
3. What is one new way you could express your gratitude through a creative outlet not yet explored? Be as specific and detailed as possible.
4. Reflect on a time when your creativity intersected with your expression of gratitude. How did it make you feel and what impact did it have on your perspective?
5. Embracing the concept of this chapter, what memories would you like to create in the future through intertwining gratitude and creativity?

CHAPTER 8

Becoming More Aware of Negative Thinking

This chapter covers the steps that are likely to be the most difficult to take because negative thinking is natural. The point isn't to entirely stop all negative thoughts because not all negative thinking is bad. Thinking negative thoughts is actually a part of human survival tactics, such as feeling pain and being able to realize that you need to act on the feeling. The worst-case scenarios can be great motivators to get yourself to a doctor to get the pain checked out. Odds are, the problem isn't going to be the worst-case scenario you considered as being possible, so you get a sense of relief as you start to treat the problem. Even if the pain indicates something serious, you are more prepared for it and have acted so that you can start trying to overcome the problem.

Negative thinking does have its place in our lives. The problem is that all too often we let negative thinking become a habit that then negatively affects us. It is so much easier to focus on the negatives than to pay attention to the positives because we tend to notice what we don't have over what we do have. This is the kind of thinking that you want to notice and put in check. You aren't going to fight negative thinking – that would be exhausting and will increase the odds that you will keep doing it. What you are doing is becoming more aware of your thought process and working to adjust it to focus on the positives. Over time, you will find that negative thoughts occur less often. This will not only help you feel better, it will make the negative thoughts that can help you actually mean more so that you are more likely to listen to and act on them.

Practice Mindfulness More Often

Once you get accustomed to being more mindful, you should start to use it as a tool to help you see when you have fallen into a repetitive negative thought pattern. There will be times when it is very obvious that mindfulness is necessary, such as when you are feeling negative emotions. There may be a very obvious source for that negativity, such as a bad day at work, but there were definitely little things that contributed and thoughts that exacerbated that negativity. When bad things happen, that's a chance to step back and put your negative thoughts spiraling downward to make you feel even worse.

Other times, you may just feel grumpy, off, or down. Stop and consider what is bringing you down and inject some of those positive thoughts. If you realize that it could be something more serious, set up an appointment with a professional. Positive thinking isn't a cure all, it is just a method of helping you live more happily and enjoy life a bit more. Mindfulness can actually help you realize when there is something more serious occurring to keep you from feeling better.

For a majority of the time and with most people, negative thinking is a result of habit, not of something more serious. Mindfulness is your best tool for noticing and adjusting your thoughts.

Mindfulness, as we have established, can provide a lifeline in the turbulent seas of negative occurrences and harmful mental patterns. With understanding in place, let's now explore the necessary practical exercises that can help navigate these difficult terrains.

1. Begin with a simple yet profound practice: conscious observation. This involves choosing any natural object

around you and focusing your entire attention on it. It could be a flower, an insect, the clouds, or even the rhythmic pattern of your own breathing. Notice the detail and intricacy. The goal is to truly see, perhaps for the first time, the object of your focus without the intrusion of judgment or labeling.

2. Another approach is to practice mindful listening. Listen to a piece of music or natural sounds like the rustle of leaves or birds singing. Pay attention to the ebb and flow of different pitches, the crescendos, the pauses. Allow the music or sound to be a pathway into the present moment.

3. Mindful immersion offers a different technique altogether. This exercise encourages you to fully engage in a simple task, resisting the urge to hurry through it to get on with the next task. It might be washing the dishes, tidying your workspace, or eating your lunch. The purpose is to shift your perspective so that the task transforms from a chore to a mindful moment full of sensory experience.

4. Body-scan meditation, an integral part of mindfulness technique, further enhances this emotional awareness. Lying down comfortably, devote a few moments to mentally scan each part of your body, from toes to head, acknowledging its presence and any sensations associated. This exercise cultivates an intimate connection with oneself, enhancing the inner awareness to deal with negative happenings.

Embarking on these journeys may feel mundane or even challenging at the beginning. But remember, this is about developing a habit, a routine. Be patient, for the essence of mindfulness lies not in the exercise itself, but in its regular practice. Over time, by harmonizing mind and body, by redirecting focus towards the present, these exercises become a natural part of how we experience and react to the world. The result is an increased awareness, a clarity of thought, and a more balanced response to negative occurrences and damaging mental patterns.

To fully appreciate how deep-seated the roots of positive thinking can go, one must first perceive the mind as a cultivated garden. Every thought is a seed, sown into the fertile soil of cognition. Think of the positive thoughts as beautiful, blossoming flowers that enrich our garden with colors and fragrance of joy, optimism, confidence, and love. Indeed, cumulatively fostering positive thoughts over time can give rise to a healthier mental state. Its influence extends through various niches of one's well-being by not only promoting resilience in the face of adversities but enhancing their overall contentment of life. Positive thinking can bring forth a cycle of goodness where positivity cultivates happiness, and happiness in turn, propagates further optimism. What we feed our minds frequently becomes our reality. When we habitually plant the seeds of positivity, we reap a mind inclined towards optimism. Over time, these individuals may handle stress better, thereby building a robust psychological immune system and enjoying a higher quality of life.

Journal Exercise:

1. Briefly describe an event from the last week where you experienced intense overt negative emotions stemming from a challenging situation.

2. How did this event progress, and did any minor negative occurrences intensify your feelings?

3. Did you immediately acknowledge the negative emotions you were feeling? If not, how long did it take you to recognize them?

4. With the perspective of mindfulness, try to identify the root cause of these emotions.

5. Write about possible positive thoughts that could have been used to offset the negativity in the moment. Reflect on how these might have altered the course of the event.

6. Do you believe your negative feelings were a result of habitual negative thinking or were they signs of a serious issue? Why?

7. Based on your observations above, define steps to implement or increase mindfulness in your daily life, particularly during challenging times.

Realize When Your Thoughts are Distorted

Distorted thinking is usually a sign of long-term negative thinking. It could be a sign that you have gotten accustomed to considering the worst-case scenario, believing that it is the one that is most likely to happen. That is almost never going to be the case, but a way of making sure you don't really appreciate the positives in your life because you are focused on the worst aspects. The following are some things to consider that can help you realize when you are working with this particular problem.

- If you regularly come up with the worst-case scenario first, and start to stop your thoughts from always going to the worst that can happen and look for something that is middle ground. If that proves to be difficult, follow up the worst-case scenario with the best-case scenario. After all, if you need to prepare for the worst result, you should also know how to prepare for the best result since they require very different responses.

  Are you frequently caught up in a vortex of 'what if' situations, predicting disastrous outcomes? The cure lies in tempering this tendency with reason. To counteract the worst-case scenario, try to:

  a) Write down the issue causing the distress, and accurately describe your catastrophic prediction.

  b) Next, weigh the evidence for and against your catastrophic prediction.

c) Consider alternative outcomes, and rate the real likelihood of each on a scale of 1-10.

d) Formulate an action plan based on these more reasonable and realistic outcomes.

Consider whether or not you look at everything in black or white. If so, you are increasing the odds that you are distorting the world around you by applying classifications that make things look much worse than they actually are. It fails to account for nuance and complexity by over-simplifying things. This works for kids because they don't understand things that are more complex, but as an adult, you should be able to recognize nuance and recognize the good and the bad of situations, and not just decide it is one way or the other.

The black or white mindset, also known as dichotomous thinking, tends to perceive situations in black and white, without any grey areas. This approach can be debilitating, as it often leads to unrealistic self-expectations and harsh self-judgment. To tackle these kinds of thoughts:

a) Recognize when you make absolute statements like 'I always fail' or 'I'll never get this right'. Jot them down and challenge them.

b) Develop a habit of thinking in spectrums. Instead of labeling a situation as a complete disaster or success, rate its quality on a scale from 1-10.

c) Practice self-compassion, and remember that learning and growth come from making mistakes.

- Realize if you are taking things personally when, most of the time, nothing personal is meant by someone's actions. If a clerk in the store doesn't smile at you while checking out your items, that isn't something personal, it usually means that the person is having a bad day on their own. You can smile at them, and maybe help give them a little something positive, but don't expect a smile back, and definitely don't ask for one. The person's actions are almost definitely not tied to you, but things they are experiencing on their own. If your kids are in a bad mood, it's probably not because of you. Odds are really good that they are dealing with their own problems, or they are undergoing biological changes (teenagers are the most notorious for this). You definitely can't take your child's mood personally, though you can sit down and talk to them to see if there is some way to help them.

Taking things personally leads to individuals perceiving events as a direct reaction to their behavior or character. It often results in substantial guilt and blame.

Combating taking things personally can be achieved by:

a) Distinguishing between your role and the roles of others in a given situation. Write these down to gain perspective.

b) Implement the broader view. Understanding that events usually have numerous contributing factors and you're not the sole influencing force.

c) Practice objective thinking and avoid jumping to conclusions by seeking additional information or viewpoints.

Journal Exercise:

1. Identify a recent situation where you remember having negative thoughts. What was the situation? Describe it in detail.

2. How did you interpret the situation at that moment? Write down the immediate thoughts and feelings you had.

3. Identify whether any of your thoughts fall under distorted thinking patterns as described in the chapter (e.g., expecting the worst outcome, oversimplifying, taking things personally).
4. Now try to reframe these thoughts from a more realistic perspective. Consider all possible outcomes, taking into account complexities and the actions of others outside of a personal context.
5. Reflect on how you feel after reframing these thoughts. Write down any changes in your feelings or perspective compared to your initial reaction.
6. What can you do in the future to recognize and correct distorted thinking earlier?

Be More Compassionate with Yourself

Most of us tend to be hard on ourselves, expecting to do better at school or work, upset about not being strong enough to get through an ordeal, or disappointed for not finishing as much work as we wanted to finish. Even if you have high expectations for yourself, you need to be more compassionate because you are just one person and can't do everything. Instead of getting upset and reprimanding yourself, practice some compassion for yourself, then use it as an opportunity to learn from what went wrong. Remember, if you fail or don't do things perfectly, that's a chance to learn, not to beat yourself up over what happened.

Frequently, the origins of internal critique stem from societal expectations and norms. We live in a society that thrives on comparison. We compare ourselves to our peers, to celebrities, and even to our own self-imposed standards. These comparisons often lead to feelings of inadequacy and a subjective sense of failure. With the advent of social media platforms, the potential for comparison and subsequent self-critique has exponentially grown. It's important to realize that the inundation of success stories, picture-perfect moments, or idealized lifestyles on such media are often curated and don't represent complete realities. Additionally, personal core values, if skewed, can be a significant source of self-criticism. An overemphasis on perfectionism or achievement, for example, can easily lead to a harsh self-evaluation. What's pivotal here is to identify these values and examine if they are truly serving your wellbeing. Redefining personal values to incorporate kindness, compassion, learning, and personal growth can mitigate the harshness of self-assessment.

When examining cognitive biases that fuel self-criticism, two prominent ones come to mind: negative filtering and overgeneralization. Negative filtering is the predisposition to focus excessively on negative aspects of ourselves or our experiences while ignoring the positive ones. Overgeneralization, on the other hand, is the propensity to extrapolate one adverse event to a pattern of continuous failure or negativity. Both these biases distort our reality and create an overly harsh perception of ourselves. Inherited beliefs from parents or caregivers also serve as significant sources of self-criticism. Sometimes, these beliefs may not be verbalized but unconsciously communicated in the form of high expectations, criticisms, or comparisons. It's crucial to note that these inherited beliefs need not continue to dictate our self-perception. They can be recognized, evaluated, and if necessary, discarded or redesigned to better serve us. Previous failure or criticism often fosters extreme self-criticism. Remembering that everyone makes mistakes and that it's a fundamental part of the human experience could potentially counteract the detrimental effects of previous failures. In essence, self-criticism can have deep-seated roots which often can be traced back to societal norms, personal values and cognitive biases. By understanding where these relentless standards come from, you will be better equipped to challenge them and embrace a more balanced, compassionate view of yourself.

Journal Exercise:

1. To start, write down 3 instances where you criticized yourself harshly for falling short of certain standards or expectations. Consider why you were so hard on yourself and reflect on how that negativity affected your mind and overall wellbeing.
2. Next, for each instance, note down alternative ways you could have reacted that would demonstrate more self-compassion. How could you have used those experiences as learning opportunities?
3. Think about a tangible instance in your day where you can consciously replace self-criticism with self-compassion. Describe how you plan to approach this experience with greater kindness towards yourself.
4. Lastly, consider how practicing self-compassion in this way might influence your future actions and reactions. How do you envision it improving your relationship with yourself, your self-esteem, and your overall attitude towards life's setbacks?

Spend Time Noticing the Positives

This suggestion has been covered before, but the time to really start noticing the positives is when you notice a stream of negative thoughts. The problem is that you have gotten into a pattern of focusing on the negatives, so you need to actively focus on the positives to counter that issue. It is much harder when you know that you are actively thinking more negative thoughts, but by this point, hopefully, you are more accustomed to encouraging positive thoughts to counter a stream of negative thoughts.

When you catch yourself in negative thoughts, use the following 5-4-3-2-1 grounding exercise, which brings your focus to the present moment and helps minimize any overwhelming feelings or thoughts.

1. Identify five things you can see around you.
2. Notice four things you can touch or feel.
3. Recognize three things you can hear.
4. Acknowledge two things you can smell.
5. Finally, think of one thing you can taste.

Journal Exercise:

1. Reflect on a situation from the past week where you had negative thoughts. Write these thoughts down.
2. Now, try to find at least three positive aspects or outcomes from that same situation. Write these down.
3. Reflect on how your perception of the situation changes when you focus on the positives rather than the negatives.
4. Write down one way you could have shifted your thinking from negative to positive during this situation, and how you plan to implement this the next time you encounter a similar scenario.
5. Finish your reflection by writing an affirmation that encapsulates your commitment to focusing on the positive in future situations.

CHAPTER 9

The Role of Relationships in Positive Thinking

Relationships, in their multifaceted forms, form the bedrock of our human experience. They shape our perspectives, influence our decisions, and often dictate our emotional states. The art of positive thinking, as emphasized throughout this book, is not just an inward journey but also about how we connect and interact with the world around us. At the core of this world are the relationships we cherish, endure, celebrate, or even regret. How we approach these relationships, influenced by the tenets of positive thinking, can drastically alter our experiences, creating ripples of positivity that extend beyond the self. Drawing parallels between the art of positive thinking and the tapestry of relationships allows us to constructively navigate our interpersonal interactions. Whether it's the unconditional love of family, the supportive nature of true friends, the intimacy of a romantic partner, the professional dynamics of the workplace, or the lessons from past relationships, each has its own set of challenges and triumphs. By embedding the principles of positive thinking, we can face these challenges head-on, celebrate the triumphs with genuine joy, and continually evolve in our journey of personal and relational growth.

Building and Sustaining Positive Family Dynamics

Instigating positive psychology in a family context is more than just a passing fad or a trendy catchphrase. It's a rigorously developed approach rooted in scientific research and practical applications that has shown tremendous potential in fostering healthier relationships, improving communication and promoting individual as well as collective happiness. Positive psychology encourages us to focus on strengths rather than weaknesses, see opportunities instead of obstacles, and invest in nurturing relationships rather than repairing them. In a family context, these principles translate to prioritizing quality interactions, active listening, empathy, open dialogue, and mutual support. Consider this, whenever there is a disagreement or a conflict, positively reframing the situation, listening actively, showing empathy, expressing feelings openly, and extending support can help rewire our approach to interpersonal issues. It nurtures an open, understanding, and supportive environment where individuals feel heard, loved, and valued thereby promoting healthier family dynamics.

1. Healthy Communication: Open the channels of communication within the family. This doesn't have to be about deep or philosophical conversations always. Even discussing ones' day, shared interests, or future plans can strengthen the emotional bond. Facilitating open and judgment-free talk about fears, aspirations, emotions, and challenges encourages the expression and understanding of diverse viewpoints and fosters collective empathy.

2. Show Empathy: Psychologists often call empathy ‚social glue' as it builds strong bonds within families. Go beyond hearing the words; try to understand the deeper emotions and perspectives. Respond with compassion and understanding, even if you disagree.

3. Spread Positivity: Acts of gratitude, appreciation, and genuine compliments can go a long way in spreading positivity. Regularly acknowledging efforts and

contributions of each member can reinforce self-esteem and increase mutual respect.

4. Mutual Support: Juggling various roles, managing professional and personal responsibilities can often get overwhelming. Offering and accepting support in any form, even a simple reassurance or words of encouragement can be significantly uplifting. It makes a person feel valued and connected.
5. Healthy Boundaries: Every individual, despite being closely associated, requires and deserves respect for personal space or boundaries. Recognizing and maintaining this can facilitate trust and mutual respect, enhancing the overall family bonding.

Journal Exercise:

1. Write down two key takeaways from the chapter.
2. Reflect on your own family dynamic. In which aspects does it relate to the concepts discussed in the chapter?
3. Identify a recurring source of tension in your family. What strategies mentioned in the chapter could you apply to navigate this tension? Write a brief action plan.
4. Recall a recent family celebration or bonding moment. How did that strengthen your family dynamics? Can you think of ways to create more such moments?
5. Jot down three aspects of your family dynamic that you cherish and would like to build upon further. How can the insights from the chapter assist in enhancing these aspects?

Friends and Positivity

The people surrounding us significantly influence our mindset, attitudes, and level of positive thinking. They say that you become the average of the five people you spend most of your time with, and if you look closely, you'll find a grain of truth in this adage. Understanding and acknowledging this impact is the first stride towards curating an environment more conducive to your growth and positivity. Judging the level of positivity in your social circle isn't trivial. Individuals exhibit nuanced behaviors, and positivity isn't always about wearing smiles or possessing an outwardly cheerful demeanor. It goes deeper than that; it is the underlying attitude towards life, resilience in the face of adversity, a growth mindset, and an inclination towards solution-oriented thinking. Observe how your friends react to setbacks. Are they quick to surrender or do they face challenges with determination and an action plan? This observation can be a reliable gauge of their outlook, and subsequently, their impact on your positivity.

Being in a social group where negativity, pessimism, and self-limiting beliefs are commonplace can unwittingly shape your thinking in the same manner. Constant exposure to such attitudes can make you adopt the same. You might find yourself shackled by a defeatist mindset, unable to fully explore your potential due to the illusion of constraints defined by your social circle. This influence operates subtly, therefore infuses into your consciousness gradually. Hence, you might not even realize that your social circle is affecting your positivity until you take a step back and evaluate it consciously. The influence doesn't stop at individual mindsets; it seeps into group dynamics as well. The unwritten rules that govern the group's behavior, commonly called 'group norms,' also impact your positivity. If the norms lean towards mutual respect, constructive feedback, and trust, they'll fuel positivity and the reverse would lead to envy, competitiveness, and negative behavior. But, every cloud has a silver lining; this principle of influence works both ways. Surrounding yourself with positive, enthusiastic individuals who cherish you and support your growth can elevate your mindset. Not only will this group inspire you to adopt a positive outlook and robust attitudes, but they will also encourage you when you falter, preventing a spiral into negativity.

Understanding that having a positive circle of friends is not about surrounding yourself with perfect people who don't have bad days, but with individuals who choose to channel even their negative circumstances into a growth experience. These are the people who will infect you with their zest for life, making your journey all the more enjoyable and nurturing the seed of positivity within you. Also, choose to be the positive influence in your circle. Bolster positive thinking and attitudes among your friends. Encourage resilience, foster a growth mindset, and promote positivity. A ripple effect will occur, creating a circle that thrives on and enhances positivity. In this shared circle of positive influence, you will grow, evolve, and become best equipped for the journey of life.

Start each day with a positive affirmation, channeling your thoughts towards an optimistic and hopeful perspective. Whether it's "Today will be a day of growth and love" or "I am a beacon of positivity who encourages joy and happiness in others," these simple words can set the tone for your interactions and your mindset. Consider your friendships as organic entities needing care, attention, and mutual respect to flourish. Bring a sense of upliftment and joy into your encounters; be the one who appreciates, compliments, and celebrates your friends' achievements. This positive reinforcement not only boosts their morale but also solidifies your bond. Moderate any negative vibrations that arise within your group with calm and sensible discussions. It's inevitable for disagreements or conflicts to occur within any social circle; what's crucial is how it is negotiated. Voice out your thoughts in a non-threatening, compassionate manner, always emphasizing the importance of unity and understanding above individual opinions. There are some simple, yet profound practices such as:

1. Maintaining a Gratitude Journal specifically for your friends - Chronicle the positive experiences you have shared with your friends and inevitable struggles that

helped you all internally grow. This journal serves as a reminder of your inter-connected growth journey.

2. Group Meditation - The practice of shared silence can have a strong impact on individual and collective positivity. This activity brings about mental equanimity, fostering a peaceful aura and cultivating mutual respect.

3. Positive Affirmation Swap - Gather your friends and write down positive affirmations tailored for each person. This habit not just boost self-esteem, but also help you to appreciate the uniqueness of each individual.

A periodic revisit of these friendships goals - perhaps through an annual getaway or just a cozy dinner - revitalizes the collective mindset toward positivity and growth. By taking stock of how far you've all come, you can look ahead with renewed commitment and joy. Remember, growth in relationships isn't merely about numbers — the years you've known each other or the number of shared good times. It's about fostering an environment where each individual feels valued, appreciated, and encouraged to be the best version of themselves. With these tools and exercises, it becomes plausible to cultivate a social environment that hums with positivity, respect, personal growth, and mutual development.

Journal Exercise:

1. List the names of five close friends who bring positivity in your life and describe the qualities that make them special.

2. Reflect on a difficult time in your life when a friend positively impacted the outcome. What did they do or say? How did it make you feel?

3. How did the insights from this chapter on ‚Friends and Positivity: Choosing the Right Circle and Growing

Together' resonate with your current friendships? Use specific examples.

4. Write a letter to your future self about the type of positive friendships you wish to cultivate and maintain. Include some steps or strategies on how to achieve this.
5. Think about a friend who could be doing better; how can you positively influence their life using the strategies outlined in this chapter? Write down these strategies and how you plan to implement them.
6. Reflect on your own qualities as a friend. What traits do you think you embody that bring positivity to your friends' lives? Where could there be room for growth or improvement?
7. What is the most valuable insight taken from this chapter and how do you plan to directly apply it to strengthen the bonds of friendship in your life?

Romantic Relationships

Positive thinking bears a significant weight in romantic relationships. When applied, it translates into an aura of hopefulness and joy that permeates through every interaction. Positive thinking invites an abundance of love and trust into relationships, primarily by fueling healthy communication, promoting understanding, and cultivating emotional intelligence. Consequently, by embracing this constructive mindset, there springs an ability to experience a higher degree of satisfaction and happiness in your relationships. Mindfulness, on the other hand, refers to the state of being present, fully focusing on what's happening, what you're doing and the space in which you're moving. By practicing mindfulness, an individual pays heed to the subtle cues that are easily neglected when engrossed in the humdrum of life. In a relationship, mindfulness manifests as active listening, expressing gratitude, practicing patience and compassion, and understanding your partner's needs and emotions. It strengthens the connection between partners, paving a clear pathway to build a lasting bond of love and trust. The third cog in this wheel is the practice of overcoming negative thoughts. Negative thought processes are a pervasive issue, affecting aspects ranging from mental health to interpersonal relationships. Negative thoughts in a relationship often stem from self-doubt, lack of confidence, past experiences, or the subconscious absorption of societal norms and standards. Inherently, these negative beliefs can cultivate fear or bitterness, undermining the love and trust in a relationship. Overcoming these thoughts can take time and often require a conscious effort, encompassing methods such as cognitive restructuring or self-affirmations.

Remember, the journey of nurturing love and trust in a relationship is not a sprint, but a marathon. It requires patience, understanding, and mutual respect. By nurturing these skills - positive thinking, mindfulness, and overcoming negative thoughts - you enhance your capacity to build meaningful and enduring relationships. It's essential to remember that the entire process is a continuous learning curve, which needs time, patience, and practice.

To make the most of effective co-evolution in your relationship, it's essential to promote positivity actively. Both partners have to develop a meticulous and practical routine. Here are some activities that can facilitate affectionate co-evolution:

1. One of the foundational practices, shared affirmation, involves speaking positive affirmations aloud to each other on a regular basis. Receiving affirmations from a loved one magnifies their effects. Furthermore, it can provide a sense of being heard and acknowledged by the other person, which greatly contributes to the goal of achieving affectionate co-evolution.

2. Journaling as a pair is a reliable practice to maintain a positive mindset and encourage growth in your relationship. It can be particularly beneficial when done together as a pair, perhaps reflecting on the day's

successes, illuminating gratitude, or illustrating hopes for future shared experiences.

3. Take time to explore your partner's hobbies and interests. This is an exceptional way to learn about your partner's dreams and passions. By taking a role in your partner's interests, both partners will likely feel more supported and understood.

4. Often, the power of surprises is underestimated. Surprising your partner with their favorite meal, an unplanned outing to a significant place, or just remembering and celebrating a meaningful yet uncommon anniversary can spark positivity.

5. Daily compliments are another surefire tactic to foster positive thinking. Complimenting your partner on their physical appearance is wonderful but focusing your compliments on their actions or their character could prove more impactful.

6. Turning disagreements into growth opportunities is a miraculous application of positive thinking in your relationship. Instead of viewing disputes as threats, asking yourself what you can learn or how you could understand your partner better can make these moments opportunities for personal and collective growth.

7. Creating common goals and projects help you to grow together. The process of working towards a shared goal involves supporting one another, understanding each other's strengths and weaknesses, and celebrating small victories. All of this enforces positivity and growth, both individually and as a pair.

Through the continuous practice of these exercises, relationships can strive towards affectionate co-evolution. What may seem like small steps have the power to build an unshakeable foundation of trust, mutual respect, and affection, all underpinned by the powerful effects of positive thinking.

Journal Exercise:

1. In this chapter, was there anything that surprised you? Write it down.
2. Reflect on the qualities you seek in a romantic relationship. Do they align with the characteristics of love, trust, and mutual growth discussed in this chapter?
3. Describe a romantic relationship - can either be yours or one you're familiar with - and analyze it through the lens of ,Cultivating Love, Trust and Mutual Growth'. In which areas does it excel? Where could it improve?
4. Recall a scenario or a conversation in your romantic relationship, which could have been handled better utilizing concepts from this chapter.
5. What is one thing from this chapter that you would like to apply to your romantic relationship? How do you plan on implementing this?
6. List down three questions about romantic relationships that you would like to explore further after reading this chapter.

Dealing with Workplace Relationships

Becoming a master of your own perspective is the first step to positively transform office politics. The reality is, office politics exist in almost every work environment. While many would perceive it as negative, you have the power to choose your response and shape such atmosphere. By cultivating a positive mindset, this seemingly negative situation becomes an arena for personal and professional growth. Let's delve into techniques that promote positive thinking, improve office communication, and ultimately produce a harmonious work environment.

1. Positive visualization is a powerful tool in building the desired work culture. Make it a habit to visualize a harmonious environment where everyone collaborates and respects each other's opinions. Creating a mental picture of the type of environment you want to work in acts as a guide, helping you react towards the goal.

2. Open communication is vital. Choosing positive words and expressing appreciation for your colleagues' efforts promotes a sense of unity, understanding, and respect. Framing criticism in a positive yet constructively critical way can motivate co-workers and stir teamwork.

3. Mindfulness aids in overcoming office politics too. Being mindful means being presently aware and objectively assessing situations without feeling overwhelmed. It allows for effective decision making and prevents engaging in any destructive office politics.

4. Among the myriad of these personal transformations, don't forget to exercise patience. Consider that changing a work culture takes time and might face resistance initially. Keep pressing forward and maintain your positivity, eventually influencing others to follow suit.

By implementing these techniques, you're not just managing office politics, but dynamically shaping it into a harmonious and productive atmosphere. Remember that the transformation starts within you. Rise above the fray of negativity to become an advocate of positivity, opening doors for a better work environment where everyone thrives.

Journal Exercise:

1. Reflect on a time you were negatively affected by office politics. What did you learn from that experience? How would the techniques outlined in this chapter have changed the outcome?
2. List three strategies from the chapter you found most helpful in developing a positive outlook towards office relationships. How can you implement these techniques in your current role?
3. Think about a positive workplace relationship you have. What elements make it successful? How can the insights from the chapter enhance this further?
4. Consider a challenging work relationship you've had or currently have. Using advice from the chapter, write a plan of action to improve this relationship and navigate office politics with a positive outlook.
5. What was your key takeaway from this chapter? Write it down and think about one way you can start applying it in your professional life from tomorrow.

Healing from Past Relationships

Each narrative of our life is like a thread, woven into one complete tapestry that depicts who we are. This includes our past relationships, which often hold a profound impact on shaping our mindset, whether we recognize it consciously or not. Unraveling the influence of past associations leads us to better understand how they mold our present psyche and behaviors. To begin this exploration, look to your patterns. Recall your past relationships and evaluate them. Consider the following: Were there certain behaviors you engaged in repeatedly? Were there similar types of people that you associated with? Did the relationships end on familiar circumstances? Identifying patterns can help you understand the type of influence past relationships have on your mindset.

1. Reflection: Identifying the patterns of your past relationships is like putting together pieces of a puzzle. By reflecting on your past, you can dissect each relationship, uncork every emotion, and learn something about yourself. Reflection can often lead to significant revelations about the causes of distinct thoughts and actions.

2. Recognize Reactions: We typically view ourselves through our reactions to situations, significant or minor. Look back at your reactions in past relationships; every physical or emotional response has the potential to reveal an ingrained mindset. Did you react with anger, frustration, avoidance, apathy, or anxiety in disputes?

3. Spot the Shadows: Past relationships can leave shadows within the mind, often lurking in the subconscious. These "shadows" can manifest as irrational fears, distrust, guilt, or a host of other emotion-based responses. Spotting these shadows and acknowledging their existence can bring them into the light and starts our journey of transformation.

Now that you have recognized patterns and reflections, it's time to transform these insights into learning experiences.

1. Reframe Negatives into Positives: Human nature tends to focus more on the negatives rather than the positives. However, each difficult circumstance is a chance for growth. If a past relationship was fraught with conflict, ask yourself what you've learned from that adversity. Did it make you more resilient? Did it make you understand the importance of clear and open communication? By reframing negatives, you can carry these lessons as positives into future relationships.

2. Self-Development and Growth: Past relationships not only affect our perceptions but they also provoke

change within ourselves. They serve as harbingers of self-development and growth. To transform the negatives, focus on nurturing habits that foster positivity, self-love, and resilience.

3. Seek Support: Sharing experiences in a safe and supportive environment can be therapeutic. Whether it's a trusted friend, a family member, or a professional therapist, external perspectives can offer insightful commentary and wisdom on your experiences.

Untying the knots of the past is never easy. However, with patience, perseverance, and understanding, you can disentangle negative influences and use them as stepping stones towards personal growth and healthier relationships. After all, who we are is often a product of where we've been.

Journal Exercise:

1. Identify one relationship in your past that you feel still affects you today. Write about your feelings associated with this relationship - both positive and negative.

2. Reflect on how this past relationship has shaped your current view of relationships. How has it impacted your behavior, attitudes, or expectations?

3. List any personal growth or lessons learnt from this relationship that have contributed to your resilience and optimism. Can you turn any negative experiences from this relationship into a positive one?

4. Write a letter to your past self in this past relationship, what would you advise or tell yourself? This is not to be sent, it's meant to be a therapeutic act of closure.

5. Now imagine your life one year from now. Write about how you would like to see yourself in terms of personal growth, relationships, and overall wellbeing. What steps can you take today to move closer to this vision?

CHAPTER 10

Maintaining Positive Thinking in Chaos and Rougher Times

The book has set you up to deal with your daily negative thoughts and gives you suggestions on how to start altering your thinking so that you have more of a positive thinking habit. It's a type of mental exercise that takes time to work. As you probably know already from doing physical exercise, there are going to be times when it is very difficult to keep exercising. Maybe you came down with the flu, so you were stuck convalescing instead of being more physically active. Maybe you got too busy and didn't have time to exercise for a while. This is going to happen with positive thinking as well. There are bound to be bad times when you aren't going to have the time or energy to work on thinking positively. It's inevitable, and that's ok. What you'll need to do is to ease yourself back into positive thinking in a way that is similar to easing yourself back into exercise.

This chapter will help you during these times, giving you what you need to keep from slipping back into a more negative thought pattern.

Give Yourself Permission to Think without Trying to Change It

There are many situations that can lead to negative thought patterns. From not making a team or organization you wanted to join to losing a job to losing a loved one, there are many reasons why you may be in a negative headspace. While you can practice some positive thinking during this time, it is perfectly fine to let yourself feel negative emotions and to let your thoughts be negative for a while. You want to avoid getting into a habit of negative thinking, but serious, negative events are going to be a legitimate reason to have negative thoughts.

Remember, when you are thinking negatively, it isn't always a bad thing. The problem is when it happens all of the time. When you have a reason to be negative, give yourself permission to have negative thoughts, as long as they aren't dangerous to you or others. If your thoughts get dark, do contact a professional. Otherwise, allow yourself a bit of time to feel those negative emotions so that you can properly process them. There will be time later to work on positive thinking when you are in a better state to think about them again.

Journal Exercise:

1. Reflect on a recent situation that caused you negative feelings or thoughts. Write down in detail what happened, how it made you feel, and the specific thoughts it invoked.

2. Observe the emotions and thoughts you've written down - do not judge or try to change them. Acknowledge them as your valid responses to the situation. How does giving yourself permission to feel negative without the need to change it affect your perception?

3. Identify what part of your experience was everyday negative thinking and if there were any darker

thoughts. If you had darker thoughts, how might you seek help or manage them better?

4. Going forward, how will you differentiate between everyday negative thoughts and harmful, dark thoughts? How can you give yourself time to process and heal from distressing events?

5. Reflect on how you can reintroduce positive thinking once you've allowed yourself adequate time to process your negative emotions. What strategies would you employ?

Remember, it's crucial not to rush or force positivity, but instead, let it naturally follow after processing your negative feelings.

Accept Help

People do better in societies than on their own, and that is because they have people around them to help. Instead of pushing people away and saying that you are alright when you aren't, accept that people are trying to help you because they have your best interests at heart. Let them help you, and you will be better able to get through the rougher times. They may be in a better mental position to help you process your emotions and see some of the positives. While you don't want other people to minimize the problem or push you when you aren't ready, a nice hug, a bit of help cleaning, or having someone to just listen to you can go a long way to helping you get back to thinking positively. You will also have something to be thankful for because you had support through a rough time.

A responsive support network of people who you can trust is crucial during times of high stress and difficulties. Your tribe will be the scaffolding that steadies you when you feel like the world is shaking. They help wrestle your worries into perspective, lightening the emotional load. To facilitate the creation of such a community, we can follow these steps, or strategies if you may:

1. Identify your People: These are individuals who encourage you, hear you without judgment, reaffirm your worth, and fill your heart with positivity. Being with them feels safe, comforting, and uplifting. Such people can be family, friends or experts like mentors, coaches, or therapists. They've shown their reliability in past situations, and you trust them. Mind you, there's a difference between those who simply make you feel good and those genuinely good for you. The latter encourages growth while relishing your happiness.

2. Reach Out: It might seem challenging, especially when you are overwhelmed, but it's vital to reach out deliberately. Let them know you need help. Share your feelings, your fears. Your tribe can only respond when they're aware of what you're grappling with. The simple act of expressing your feelings is cathartic in itself. Further, it creates an opportunity for potential solutions or alternate perspectives that you may have overlooked.

3. Regular Interaction: Keep your tribe close, even when the storm passes. Regular interaction helps form stronger bonds, ensures you're aware of each other's situations, and enables easier communication during crises. Whether it's a quick chat or meaningful conversations over a meal - be proactive in maintaining these relationships.

4. Virtual Support: If physical meeting is a challenge, especially with today's risk of spreading viruses from social gatherings, there are several online resources you can leverage. Many mental health apps provide support groups that can aid in overcoming stress and other mental health issues. Additionally, there are several online platforms offering guidance, therapy, and words of encouragement. Do not limit yourself only to physical boundaries.

5. Nurture Versatility within Your Network: It's useful to have a varied network - different friends for different needs. Some may be excellent at providing solutions, others at empathy, and still others at diversion. Respect what each person brings to your life and leverage that in times of need. Remember, there's no one-size-fits-all, and this applies to your support network too.

6. Additionally, explore environments conducive to tranquility or productivity; it could be a quiet corner in a library, a park bench, or a favorite coffee shop. The right environment can work wonders in restoring equilibrium. Surround yourself with positivity that foster's optimism, healing elements like fresh air, pleasant music, uplifting artworks - all these elements are intrinsic in curbing overwhelming feelings.

Journal Exercise:

1. Reflect on the last time you accepted help from someone during a difficult time. How did it make you feel?

2. Identify three people in your life that you trust and who you could ask for help if needed. List the ways they could assist you.

3. Describe a situation when you rejected help from others. What held you back from accepting it? How did it affect your situation and mindset?

4. How could you be more open to accepting help in the future?

5. Write a note of gratitude to someone who offered you help during a challenging time. Acknowledge the value of their support and how it positively impacted your mindset.

Practice Your Favorite Positive Thought Activities

As you process negative emotions, you can resort to the activities that you enjoyed doing the most. Maybe you enjoyed journaling, in which case, start doing that again, even if you are expressing your negative thoughts. Since you are accustomed to adding positive thoughts, it will be easier to start adding them earlier in the process as you process events.

If you are busy and life is chaotic without a single event making it difficult, modify your favorite activities so that you can do them when you are on the go. Maybe you can't sit and keep a journal to work on your thoughts because life is too chaotic. Start creating voice messages in the same style as your journaling because this can be done while you are stuck in traffic, are waiting for kids to finish an activity, or while you are at the airport. If you enjoy daily affirmations and find that it's too exhausting to do a lot of additional thinking after a series of long days, talk to someone and see if they can offer you some positive thoughts about yourself. It isn't fishing for compliments. It is getting an outside perspective to remind you of the positives when you are too drained to do it yourself.

Journal Exercise:

1. Reflect on the current challenges you are facing. In what areas are you finding it hardest to maintain a positive perspective?

2. Write about one or two activities that you usually cherish but have found challenging to partake in during these harder times. How can you adjust these activities to suit your current situation?

3. Think about a recent instance when you were feeling down. How could you have incorporated a favorite positive thought activity to navigate through that situation?

4. Record a five-minute voice memo about your day and the activities you've done to maintain positivity. What are the thoughts that come up as you do this?
5. Reflect on the people or relationships in your life that provide you encouragement and positive reinforcement. How has their input helped you maintain positivity during rough times?

Exercise Mindfulness and Your Body

Physical exercise is just as good for your mental state as it is for your body. When you are feeling stressed, restless, overwhelmed, or upset, make time in your schedule to go do an activity that will work your body, giving your mind time to finally relax from everything else. Yes, this will be hard because if things are chaotic we can easily excuse not taking time to exercise. Don't let yourself do this though. When you are stressed, this is the best time to exercise your mind and body because it forces a much-needed break.

If you still continue to exercise, shift that time to do something you don't usually do so that you aren't following the same schedule. The point is to switch things up a bit so that your body and mind have a chance to have a different experience to better process all of the stress and hectic schedule. It will go a long way toward helping to make things feel easier to manage.

The scientific community has long celebrated the correlation between physical activity and mental well-being. Upon physical exertion, our body produces endorphins - neurotransmitters responsible for a sense of happiness and euphoria. These 'feel-good' hormones can significantly reduce feelings of stress and anxiety, and increase our overall emotional resilience. By participating in regular physical activities during difficult times, an individual can foster a resilient mindset, remain focused, and create a buffer against daily stresses. Incidentally, physical activity is two times as effective when combined with mindfulness. Mindfulness—

an act of maintaining a moment-to-moment awareness of our thoughts, feelings, bodily sensations, and the surrounding environment has a therapeutic effect on our psychology. It increases our awareness of our thoughts and feelings, reduces impulsive reactions, and improves decision-making skills. When combined with physical activity, it amplifies the psychological benefits twofold.

Here's how this combination works:

1. Stress Reduction: Physical activities like yoga, tai-chi, or even simple stretches that incorporate mindfulness can lower the production of stress hormones like cortisol. As a result, an individual is likely to feel calmer and more at peace even amidst a turbulent situation.

2. Heightened Self-awareness: Mindful physical activities enable us to pay better attention to our bodily sensations. We become more in tune with ourselves, understanding our body's reactions better, thus leading to improved self-awareness.

3. Mental Fortitude: The combination of mindfulness and physical activity leads to improved mental fortitude. It helps to build mental grit and resilience-an important trait to navigate through tough times.

4. Positive Mindset: A consistent practice of mindful physical activity can lead to cognitive restructuring, meaning, it can help in reshaping our thought patterns. It promotes positive thinking, thus improving general well-being and happiness.

5. Improved Focus and Concentration: Physical activity requires focus and concentration, and especially when combined with mindfulness, increases our ability to concentrate. This improved focus can spill over into other areas of life, aiding us in overcoming challenges more effectively.

6. Shared Experiences and Social Connection: Participating in group exercises which involve mindfulness, like group yoga classes, can cultivate a

sense of community and shared experience, fostering feelings of belonging and positivity.

Physical activity intertwined with mindfulness not only ensures a healthy body but also cultivates a resilient and positive mind. By embracing this holistic approach, a tumultuous period can be transformed into a period of personal growth and self-discovery. Therefore, navigating through challenges can become easier, with a newfound ability to bounce back, remaining positive, and taking things in stride. This, in a nutshell, reflects our inherent human strength. By allocating a certain period of your day to focusing on your wellbeing, you create an island of tranquility in the sea of chaos that often punctuates day-to-day existence. Although we covered some of them already before, here are several simple yet highly effective techniques you can incorporate into your daily routine:

1. Morning positivity affirmations: Start your day by stating positive affirmations. This simple technique is particularly effective in setting the tone for the day. It is as simple as looking at yourself in the mirror every morning and uttering reassuring statements like, „I am capable“, „This will be a good day“, „I am stronger than my challenges,“ and so on. This can be a significant morale booster and give you the strength to face the chaos of life head on.

2. Visualization: Take a few moments every day to visualize a serene, peaceful landscape - a calm beach, a tranquil forest, or a quiet mountaintop. Visualization techniques allow you to create a sense of calm within yourself that you can fall back upon during chaotic times. You can try doing this activity in the morning or just before going to bed.

3. Breathing exercises: Simple breathing techniques have proven to be extremely effective in calming the mind. Start by taking slow, deep breaths. Focus on the sensation of breath entering and leaving your nostrils. Push out all external thoughts and concentrate on your inhale and exhale. This technique can be used

anywhere, and at any time, when you feel overwhelmed, and it'll help you to center your thoughts.

4. Yoga or fitness routines: Physical activity is extremely beneficial in managing stress and chaos. Try to include a simple yoga or fitness routine as part of your daily tasks. Choose a convenient time for yourself, be it in the morning or the evening. Include basic exercises like stretching, push-ups and squats. Such practices release endorphins, the feel-good hormones, and help you to start or end your day on a positive note.

5. Gratitude Journaling: At the end of each day, write down at least one thing that you are grateful for. This encourages positive thinking, especially in times of distress, and reminds us of the good things in life that often get overlooked in times of chaos.

6. Regular breaks: Regular breaks are integral to maintaining equilibrium. They can be as short as 5 minutes but do something that will take your mind off work or other stressors. You could go for a quick walk, have a healthy snack, or listen to your favorite music.

The beauty of these exercises and mindfulness techniques is in their flexibility. These can be modified as per individual comfort and convenience. Some days will be harder than others, and it is essential to remember that it's okay not to follow them religiously. The critical aspect is to remain consistent, disciplined, and patient with oneself. Progress may not be overnight, but it surely will be worth it.

Journal Exercise:

1. Reflect on a time when you were faced with chaos or rough times. How did it affect your mental and physical health? Write down a brief summary of that experience.

2. Based upon what you've learned in the chapter, list down three ways on how practicing physical activity

could have potentially aided you during this difficult period.

3. Do you currently have a physical activity routine? If yes, describe what includes. If no, write down a simple yet effective routine you'd want to start following.
4. Describe a new physical activity you'd like to try based upon what you've read in the chapter. Explain your reasons why you chose this specific activity and how you think it might benefit your state of mind during difficult times.
5. Reflect on the importance of maintaining positive thinking in times of chaos. Write a personal commitment about how you plan to prioritize physical exercise in your routine, especially during stressful periods.
6. Lastly, anticipate any obstacles that might prevent you from sticking to your routine. Develop a solution for each potential hurdle. Remember, the aim is not only to exercise the body, but to exercise mindfulness.

Seek out Positivity

Ironically, social media is probably the best way to seek out positivity. Avoid sites that you know may exacerbate negative thoughts. Avoid true crime, how-tos, and sites that will force your thoughts in certain directions. You don't want to think about crimes and negative events in life, nor do you want to see people who look happy showing you how you *should* be doing things.

No, this is the time to seek out what is considered mindless fun. Watch animal videos, clips of puppies just being adorable, or children doing things that make you shake your head and laugh. Look for light subjects that are more likely to make you smile despite everything going on around you. It doesn't matter how hectic and busy you are, you need to have a reason to smile and laugh, and these adorable and funny sites will help you do just that.

Journal Exercise:

1. Reflect on any recent times when you found yourself drawn into negative content online or on social media. How did it affect your mood or perspective?
2. Write down three things you can do to actively seek out more positive content. It could be as simple as subscribing to a ‚good news' channel or following an artist that you admire.
3. Think about a time when you stumbled upon a piece of uplifting content (like a funny video or an inspirational quote) that improved your mood. Describe how it made you feel and why.
4. Develop a mantra for yourself to refocus your attention when you feel drawn towards negative content. Write this mantra down and commit to using it when necessary.
5. Record the effect using these actions has on your mindset over the course of a week; do you notice a difference in your positivity levels?

CHAPTER 11

Tips and Tricks to Keep You Going

Similar to doing exercises, you are going to find there are times when you just don't want to put in the effort to think positively. You don't need to have a significant negative event or a hectic schedule to make it difficult to think positively. Sometimes the season can bring you down, with winter being too cold and dark and summer being too hot to get outside. It could be a series of minor negatives that just build up over time, or it could be just a couple of days where you really feel grumpy. There are a lot of minor things that can interfere with positive thinking, even if you have been doing it for years.

You may not be at a high risk of falling back into a pattern of negative thinking, but you really don't want to take a chance on doing that. This chapter gives you a few tips and tricks to encourage positive thinking, even when you have a desire to just sit and wallow for a bit. It is ok to pout for a couple of minutes or to let yourself be unhappy for a couple of minutes – happiness is stressful – but you want to make sure that your mind doesn't get stuck there. Here are the tips and tricks to return to the positive frame of mind that will help get you out of the negative emotions a bit faster.

Get out in nature

This is an old reliable way of helping to clear your mind and stop feeling negative because there is so much in nature that just distracts you from the thoughts in your head. All seasons offer something amazing and distracting that will pull you out of your head and force you into the present. You will find it far easier to think positively when you are out in nature because of how beautiful it can be.

Maybe the best you can manage is to be grateful that you finally get to go back inside. Even that is something positive for those who aren't outdoor enthusiasts. Getting into nature doesn't mean driving a long distance either. Find a nearby park where you've never gone or where you haven't been recently and visit it. Stroll around the neighborhood. Whatever you can do to get outside and shake up your mindset is going to be beneficial.

Given that there are times of the year where this may not be possible (when there is 8 feet of snow outside or it is 100 degrees, going outside isn't exactly realistic), there are still plenty of things you can do to help improve your mental state.

Nature offers many special moments that will benefit your well-being. Observing the sun rising or setting each day is one of them. It not only offers an awe-inspiring visual, but also brings a feeling of freshness and starting anew when it rises and a feeling of completeness when it sets. This could be an excellent way to start or finish your day with decisiveness, acknowledging the cycle of existence, the importance of every moment, and the transitory nature of time. Make this a habit - begin your day with just ten minutes in the sunshine, soaking in its rays, grounding yourself, and harnessing positive energy for the day. On a more scientific note, sunshine contributes to the body's production of Vitamin D - a deficiency of which is linked to feelings of depression. By ensuring that you get just a little sunshine every day, you're helping keep your body healthy and your spirits high.

Nature's brilliance is not confined to only sunshine; let's dive deeper into the realm of flora, or plants. Besides the oxygen plants produce, having them within your environment has been shown to reduce stress, increase feelings of contentment, and improve cognitive function. You might not have the ability to walk in a forest every day; nevertheless, introducing small houseplants to your space can mimic these effects. Remember the power of touch - feeling the texture of tree barks, the smoothness of pebbles, or the softness of petals. Use this opportunity to explore different sensations and refocus your thoughts and attention to the present moment.

Fresh air, or more simply, the act of breathing can be an excellent tool to check our current state of mind. Diaphragmatic or deep belly-breathing is a technique used in many forms of meditation and yoga. When feeling stressed or lost in your thoughts, venture outside and gather clean, fresh air. Fill your lungs and try to exhale any negativity or tension you may be holding. Practicing this method regularly acts as an anchor to free your mind and to rid of any mental rubbish. A similar effect can be achieved by stepping out during the evening and gazing at the stars. The vastness of space and time, the mysterious unknown, can put our troubles into perspective. Also fauna: observing animals and wildlife. Birds chirping, a squirrel's bustling activities, movements of fishes in a pond - observing these small wonders can serve as gentle reminders that we are part of a larger ecosystem. Interacting with animals, where possible, is another great way of relieving stress and promoting positive thoughts.

Every element of nature has the capacity to soothe our minds and stimulate positivity. It's a matter of developing awareness and incorporating these factors daily. Spread your attention across the four elements: observe the morning sunshine, take care of a plant, enjoy the fresh air, or watch a happy dog running. Connect with nature and reconnect with your authentic self.

Especially when living in cities, it can be difficult to connect to Nature. However, here are three tips that might help you, if you're living in a city:

1. Indoor plants: An excellent conduit to connect with nature on an everyday basis. Houseplants not only add a dash of color and freshness to your interiors, they also act as natural air purifiers. English Ivy, Snake Plant, and Peace Lily are great for this purpose. Taking care of these plants becomes a nurturing exercise, teaching us patience and mindfulness. There are numerous plants that thrive indoors with minimal attention. It is important, however, to choose the right kind of plants basis the sunlight and humidity conditions of your place. Remember, tending to your indoor garden can become your meditative routine, guiding your focus back to the present moment, while you're trimming, watering, or potting these vibrant gifts of life.

2. Why not create mini-green spaces within your premises? A small terrace or a balcony can easily be converted into your mini oasis. Use this space to grow some herbs, eatables, or flowering plants. If you lack outdoor space, windowsills make for perfect spots for your herb garden. Explore vertical gardening for walls and fences. Objects from daily use like mason jars, old tires, or even shoe racks can be repurposed into planters adding an extra dash of creativity and sustainability to your venture. Bird-feeders make a beautiful addition to such space. The idea is to create a mini-ecosystem, which will not only serve you fresh, home-grown produce, but also act as a retreat where you can spend a few quiet moments every day, thus promoting inner peace.

3. Be in tune with weather changes. Each season unravels a different face of Mother Nature. Take a moment to acknowledge and appreciate this. Enjoy the warm sunlight on your skin in winters, the cool breeze during summers, or the pattering rain on your windowpane. Unleashing the sensory experiences related to weather changes can be a simple yet profound practice of

mindfulness. You see, between the concrete structures and high-rises, our cities are full of such beautiful experiences waiting to be acknowledged, only if we know where to look.

Urban environments can often be overwhelming with concrete structures, pollution, and noise. However, if we can, within this chaos, unravel a connection with nature, not only can we make our dwellings healthier and more beautiful, but we may also realize that the essence of well-being resides within our reach. Each day, make an effort to appreciate the miracles of nature, whether it's a new leaf on your rose plant, a bird visiting your feeder, or the rain creating ephemeral art on your window. Incorporating Mother Nature into your daily routine can be a rewarding journey of rediscovery, mindfulness, and deep joy. Remember, no space is too small, no routine is too packed, to find room for Nature and its serenity.

Journal Exercise:

1. Describe a time when being outside in nature uplifted your mood. What specific elements of the environment contributed to this feeling?
2. What is your preferred season for enjoying nature? How does this season affect your senses and emotions compared to other seasons?
3. If you are usually indoors, what potential benefits could you perceive if you incorporate nature time into your routine? How could you feasibly make that change?
4. Consider a time when bad weather made it impossible to go outside. What alternative methods did you use to uplift your mental state?

Indulge in a Small Guilty Pleasure

We spend a lot of time policing ourselves and making sure that our time is spent well or that we get all of the chores done. Do something that you don't usually get to do instead of something that you would usually do. This doesn't mean playing hooky or committing a crime. Instead of doing the dishes immediately after your meal, go do something you want to do. Sometimes all you need is to feel like you have done something for you – and only for you – to help you feel better about things.

Naturally, this should not become an activity you do regularly. The fact that you occasionally let yourself watch a show that you know is junk, ignore the chores for an afternoon, or take a break from life for an evening will help you feel more positively. This is particularly effective when you feel like you are in a rut. Giving yourself permission to ignore less critical responsibilities for a little bit to do something you want to do reminds you that there is plenty of fun to be had, you just have to get to a point where you can do it more often. Guilty pleasures are things that you can't usually indulge in, so giving yourself permission to be a little irresponsible and do them is a real boost for your mental state when things feel stale.

However, there arises a question of significant import: how does one maintain balanced indulgence? A three-pronged approach can be proposed, involving recognizing needs, establishing boundaries, and allowing exceptions.

Recognizing these indications of needing indulgence: feeling stressed, overworked, or emotionally drained, are signs of requiring a recreational distraction to recalibrate one's mental equilibrium. Heeding them can lead to preventative indulgence, which in turn, can be surprisingly beneficial.

Establishing boundaries should be the next step. Conversing with oneself about what constitutes a 'healthy indulgence', how often, and in what quantities it should be practiced, can be helpful. Instilling these boundaries submits indulgence to the conscious mind, instead of it being an impulsive act.

Rigidity can lead to the creation of another stress source and thus, permitting exceptions becomes crucial. Should you find yourself yearning to indulge outside the fixed boundaries, instead of shunning the idea outright, question it. If the desire stems from needing stress relief, or is a result of achieving a milestone, yielding to it might prove more beneficial than harmful.

More than likely, negative thoughts often stem from focusing on mistakes or failures. Each time you indulge correctly, positivity is bolstered. Beyond that, it's important to frame indulgences—and the occasional over-indulgence—in positive light. Mistakenly over-indulging is not a failure, but a learning experience that encourages development of better strategies to approach indulgence.

Thus, the journey towards reaping the beneficial effects of occasional indulgences and minimizing the negative ones hinges on recognizing the need, setting boundaries, allowing exceptions when needed and maintaining positive thinking. As with any self-improvement exercise, patience and persistence can make this endeavor a rewarding one.

In order to maintain an optimized and balanced life, it is essential to integrate smart strategies for indulging your guilty pleasures. Follow these practical exercises and methods to do so:

1. Set Clear Boundaries: Determine the limits of your indulgence upfront. Whether it's a scoop of ice cream or an hour playing video games, ensure this limit is not exceeded. Hold yourself accountable and it‘s equally essential not to give in to the ‚just one more‘ temptation. This way, your guilty pleasure remains an occasional treat, not an unhealthy habit.
2. Time Management: Allocate specific time slots for your guilty pleasures. This might mean you get your treat at

the end of each week or even each day, depending on the activity itself. The key here is to not let it eat into your productive time. Having a designated time will both give you something to look forward to and will prevent overindulgence.

3. Group it with a Healthy Habit: Pair your guilty pleasure with a positive task. For example, combine your favorite TV show with folding laundry or allow yourself a piece of chocolate after a brisk walk. This will make indulgence more rewarding and you will end up creating a productive routine.

4. Transform it into a Reward: Use your guilty pleasure as a reward for achieving a specific goal. Have you finished a challenging project before the deadline? Reward yourself with a 15-minute break to scroll through social media. This method ensures that your pleasure becomes part of a reward system, strengthening your motivation to complete tasks efficiently.

5. Mindful Indulgence: Fully immerse yourself in the experience when you are indulging. If it's food, savor every bite; if it's a hobby, immerse yourself in the activity completely. Being fully present will increase your enjoyment and satisfaction, reducing the likelihood of over-indulgence.

6. Controlled environment: Remove the triggers in your surroundings that lead to over-indulging. If you know you are likely to eat an entire bag of chips, don't buy it in the first place. Opt for a single serving, so you cannot overindulge even if you wanted to.

These practices can guide you in enjoying your guilty pleasures without them steering into the territory of unhealthy habits. Over time, you'll find yourself looking forward to these indulgences, making them a positive aspect of your overall lifestyle. Remember, the key is balance. Guilty pleasures are not something to eradicate entirely but to embrace smartly. Through mindful indulgence, you can harmonize relaxation and productivity, adding joy and flavor to your everyday life.

Practicing these steps consistently will help transform your relationship with your guilty pleasures from a source of guilt to a source of motivation and well-being.

Journal Exercise:

Reflect on a personal guilty pleasure that you occasionally indulge in but never really took notice of. How often do you allow yourself to take part in it? What feeling does it evoke in you? Do you think there is a risk of it becoming a habit? If there are no guilty pleasures, why not? How can you introduce one to your routine in a way that is beneficial and non-intrusive to your responsibilities? Can you identify ways in which this guilty pleasure might serve as an antidote to periods where you feel stuck or overwhelmed? Write down these thoughts and consider the balance you maintain between life's work and its joys.

Try Something New

Often the problem that causes a stream of negative emotions is a sense of boredom, lack of purpose, or just feeling like we do the same thing all of the time. If you feel too guilty to be a little irresponsible for a short period of time, or if you don't have time for guilty pleasures (parents often don't), find something new to try. This can be as simple as finding a new recipe that you want to try. Maybe you get inspiration from something you've seen on TV, such as Kronk's spinach puffs in *The Emperor's New Groove*, and you are curious if you can come up with a similar dish. You can involve other people in the effort, creating an entertaining experience as you work through the new activity, recipe, or product.

Contrary to popular belief, comfort zones aren't just about physical spaces or routine. It encompasses our thoughts, behaviors, and reactions too. When we dare to challenge these embedded patterns, we pave the way for personal growth. It is akin to exercising mental muscles, making them more pliable, agile, and capable, all the while fostering a sense of confidence and self-assurance. The more we push these boundaries, taking calculated risks and experiencing unfamiliar circumstances, the more we expand our potential. Researchers have found that novelty sparks our curiosity and enhances our learning capacity. It creates what psychologists call "state of optimal anxiety". In moderation, this anxiety can stimulate our cognition, making us more receptive to knowledge and new experiences. Furthermore, when we conquer fresh challenges, we increase our psychological resilience. It familiarizes us with the pattern of overcoming adversity, making us tougher in the face of future difficulties. It's the classic theory of 'what doesn't kill us makes us stronger' applied to our mental fortitude.

Journal Exercise:

1. Reflect on a time when you experienced feelings of monotony in your life. What did you do to combat these feelings? If faced with a similar situation again, would you do anything differently?
2. Identify an activity or area of life you have been meaning to introduce some novelty to but haven't yet. Why have you been putting it off? What barriers, if any, are there to trying something new in this area?
3. Based on the insights gained from this chapter, devise an action plan for trying out a new hobby, action, or experiment. Be sure to include the following:
    - The activity you've chosen
    - The steps you'll take to get started
    - Any resources you need or challenges you anticipate
    - How this new activity aligns with combating feelings of monotony

4. Consider any potential collaborations – who in your life would enjoy this activity? How could they enrich the experience?

5. As you try your new activity based on the action plan, reflect on your mood before and after the activity. Did the change from your routine rejuvenate you? How did the experience compare to your initial expectations?

Indulge in Music

Putting in earplugs and listening to music can be incredibly liberating because it blocks out the world around you. You need to make sure that you are listening to music that is upbeat to help improve your mood and thoughts, but music has repeatedly proven to be an exceptionally effective way of helping to change a person's emotions. Even if you can't listen with earplugs, playing upbeat music in your home can help you feel a lot better. If you end up with something that gets you moving around and dancing a bit, all the better since you are improving your mental state through both more bodily movement and positive music.

Music, in many ways, speaks a universal language. Its powerful influence on our emotions isn't just a fleeting feeling but has deep-rooted connections in neuroscience. The rhythm and tones of music can activate multiple areas of the brain, including those responsible for memory and emotion. It's no wonder that a familiar tune can transport us back to a specific moment in time, invoking vivid memories and emotions. The beauty of music lies in its versatility. While upbeat songs can inject joy and enthusiasm, slow and melodic tunes can offer solace and tranquility. If you're feeling restless or anxious, try listening to classical music or instrumental tracks. The harmonious blend of instruments can have a calming effect, reducing stress and promoting relaxation. On the other hand, if you're feeling low or lethargic, pop, rock, or even dance tracks can give that needed boost of energy, motivating you to take on challenges head-on. Creating personalized playlists for different moods can be an effective strategy. For instance, a 'Morning Motivation' playlist could include songs that invigorate and inspire you to start your day right, while an 'Evening Relaxation' list might feature calming tracks to help you wind down.

It's also beneficial to explore different genres and cultures of music. Every culture has its unique rhythm and tunes that capture its essence. Listening to international music can not only introduce you to diverse melodies but can also foster a sense of connection and understanding of global cultures. This can be particularly uplifting, as it broadens your musical horizons and deepens your appreciation for the art form. Moreover, singing along to your favorite tunes can amplify the positive effects of music. It's a form of self-expression that allows you to release pent-up emotions, whether it's the joy of hitting those high notes or the catharsis of belting out heartfelt lyrics. If you play an instrument, spending some time playing your favorite melodies can be therapeutic. Engaging with music actively, rather than just passively listening, can heighten the emotional experience. Sharing music is another beautiful aspect that can enhance your well-being. Swap playlists with friends or family, or introduce them to a new artist or track you've discovered. Such shared experiences can lead to deeper connections, and there's a unique joy in witnessing someone else appreciate a piece of music you love. In essence, music isn't just a background score to our lives; it's an active participant. It carries the power to elevate our moods, heal wounds, and connect us on a profound level. By making music a regular part of your routine and exploring its vast spectrum, you ensure a reservoir of positivity and energy that you can tap into whenever needed. So, the next time you feel out of sorts or need a pick-me-up, let the melodies guide you, and lose yourself in the transformative magic of music.

Journal Exercise:

1. Write down three songs that inspire, uplift, or elevate your mood whenever you listen to them. What are the specific elements in these songs that make you feel

this way? Is it the lyrics, beat, melody, or the memories associated with them?

2. Think of a moment when you felt down or unmotivated and a specific song altered your mood. Describe that experience. Do you often use music as a coping mechanism for unpleasant emotions?

3. Imagine you are tasked with creating a playlist for someone going through a tough time and needs uplifting. List out at least five songs you would include and explain why you chose these particular tracks.

4. Write about a time when a song made you get up and dance. How did it affect your overall mood and physical well-being?

5. Moving forward, how do you plan to incorporate more music into your daily routine for better mental and physical well-being? Could there be specific times or activities where music can enhance your experience or mood?

Pay Attention to What You Are Consuming in the Digital World

We all have our favorite YouTube, Twitch, and other digital sites, as well as podcasts and other digital areas. If you are paying attention to sites or programs that tend to be negative, such as true crime, scary stories, unsolved mysteries, rants, or other negative emotions, take a break from them. Ignore your notifications and actively look for things that will help inspire positive thinking. This can be how-tos, especially if you are interested in taking up a particular activity, because it may be possible to make time for it in your schedule. The news is another source of negativity that too many of us follow. Since you really can't ignore the news, make sure that you balance it with positive media. You need to make sure that you are consuming more positive digital information than negative to help you think more positively about life. There will always be negative things to learn, and we are prone to focusing on them instead of the positives. When you are more aware of your own inclinations to negative media, you can start adjusting it so that you are seeing some positives to remind yourself that there is a lot of good out there too – it just generally isn't as sensational and doesn't get as many clicks. You can help change your pattern so that people start to offer more positives in this particular sphere.

Quality and timing of digital consumption can have a profound impact on our lives, often subtly influencing our mindset and overall wellbeing. Therefore, managing digital consumption, just like any other area of our wellness, is a skill that can be developed. Have you ever noticed, that some days, you feel down without any particular reason? Look closer. Often, it's your digital diet - what you watch, read, and absorb from the world through your phone or laptop. For instance, mindlessly scrolling through a flood of negative news can leave us feeling anxious, while being barraged with polished images on social media might intensify feelings of insecurity. Therefore, what we need is a balanced digital diet - a mix of content that informs, inspires, educates, and entertains us. Here are a few actionable tips:

1. Diversify your sources: Don't rely on a single platform or source for your news or information. Explore different perspectives to get a more complete picture of the world.

2. Actively search for uplifting content: Positive content can uplift our mood. Incorporate it in your digital diet to initiate a shift in your mindset.

3. Limit exposure to toxic or distressing content: It's vital to be aware of what's happening in the world, but over-exposure to negative news can lead to a phenomenon called ‚doomscrolling' and associated psychological distress.

Also the timing of what part of the day you are engaging in the digital world is an important part of well-being. Recent studies reveal that the timing of our digital consumption significantly influences our mood and productivity. Here are three steps to balance the timing:

1. Establish ‚Digital Sunsets': It's beneficial to have at least an hour of technology-free time before bed, considering the impact of screen light on the quality of sleep.
2. Practice ‚Mindful Mornings': Begin the day with purposeful activities that fuel positivity instead of immediately reaching out for the phone.
3. Take Regular ‚Digital Detoxes': Schedule regular short breaks from technology throughout the day, and longer breaks over the weekends or holidays to rejuvenate.

By consciously choosing the type of digital content we consume, and setting thoughtful boundaries on when we consume it, we can significantly improve our mental and emotional health. It's like building your very own digital sanctuary, a pleasant, friendly environment, which can contribute significantly to nurturing a more positive and balanced mindset. This is not about abandoning technology. Instead, it is about learning to use it in ways that fuel our wellbeing rather than drain it. Ultimately, the journey towards digital wellness is a personal one, requiring continuous self-awareness, adjustment and balance. However, remember that even small steps can cause ripples of change. Start simple, start small, and prepare to feel a difference. Recognizing the influence of online content on our psyche is crucial, as it's akin to understanding the food we consume and the impact on our physical wellbeing. Emotional intelligence is a key tool in discerning the potentially intoxicating draw of digital content, enabling us to navigate the vast expanses of information in a healthy and constructive manner. A hallmark of emotional intelligence is self-awareness, equipping individuals to better perceive the effects of digital consumption on their mental state.

It is through perceptiveness, a vital component of emotional intelligence, that we can begin to understand these effects. Regularly self-monitoring our emotional states after digital consumption allows us to map out patterns of emotional response. What content leaves us feeling bewildered, drained, or uneasy? Conversely, what content provides us with joy, peace, or thought-provoking insights? The following disciplinary traits of emotional intelligence are:

1. Control: The ability to retain cognitive mastery even amid volatile emotional states is pivotal. We must avoid being consumed by the digital world. It‘s crucial to realize that online content is controllable and not let it control us.

2. Empathy: How are the emotions, thoughts, and experiences conveyed in the digital content affecting us? Whose voices are we letting into our emotional landscape? What narratives are we subscribing to? It‘s essential to assess these questions in understanding our emotional responses.

3. People Skills: Communication in the digital realm is not limited to broadcasting our thoughts. It also involves listening and providing appropriate responses. This attentiveness affects our emotional equilibrium and influences how we interact online.

Journal Exercise:

1. Reflect on your typical online consumption for a day. What type of content do you mainly expose yourself to?

2. How would you rate your digital content in terms of positivity and negativity? Write down the examples of positive and negative digital content that you consume on a regular day.

3. Identify and describe any changes in your moods, feelings or thoughts that you notice after exposure to negative online content.

4. Identify and describe how you feel after exposure to positive digital content.

5. What strategies can you put in place right now to draw your attention away from negative digital content and towards positive?
6. Reflect on how implementing these strategies may benefit your overall mental and emotional well-being.
7. Looking ahead, write down your commitment for a positive digital consumption pattern. What are some uplifting and instructional content you wish to engage with more?
8. At the end of the week, reflect on your journey of transforming your digital consumption. Note the challenges you encountered and how you navigated them. Write down any changes in your feelings, mood, and mindset attributable to this shift.

CHAPTER 12

Conclusion: The Everlasting Journey of Positive Thought

As we approach the culmination of this guide, it's essential to reflect on the journey you've embarked upon. The pathway to positive thinking isn't a destination but rather a continual process, much like the ebb and flow of tides. By now, you've acquired tools and insights into mindfulness, emotional intelligence, and the intricacies of maintaining a positive mindset. However, knowledge is just the beginning. The real transformation begins when you apply this knowledge daily, adapting and evolving with life's challenges. In this final chapter, we will explore the importance of crafting a forward-looking vision and ensuring that the principles of positive thinking remain a lifelong commitment.

Crafting a Positive Vision for Tomorrow

This journey has been a voyage of introspection, understanding, and most importantly, change. But every journey, no matter how enlightening, must find its conclusion. And what better way to conclude than by crafting a vision for tomorrow, steeped in the positivity you've cultivated? Reflect upon the insights gained, the tools acquired, and the strategies discussed. They're not just isolated chapters in a book but milestones on a path you're paving for a brighter, more optimistic future. The end of this guide isn't an ending at all – it's a new beginning. It's a pledge to yourself to carry forward the lessons learned and to apply them in every facet of your life. Tomorrow is a canvas of endless possibilities. But unlike an artist who starts with a blank slate, you now possess a palette rich with shades of positivity, emotional intelligence, and mindfulness. Your strokes, influenced by affirmations and a keen awareness of your emotional landscape, will paint a picture that resonates with hope, resilience, and joy.

Yet, as with any art, the beauty lies in its evolution. The vision you craft for tomorrow will evolve, change, and mature as you do. There will be challenges, of course, moments of doubt and uncertainty. But armed with the insights from this journey, you'll view them not as insurmountable obstacles but as opportunities for growth. In conclusion, as you stand on the brink of tomorrow, remember this: the tools and techniques in this guide are your allies. Lean on them, refine them, and integrate them into your daily life. Let them guide you as you craft a vision for tomorrow that is both radiant and filled with positive promise. And as you do, take a moment to appreciate the journey thus far, and the beautiful horizon that awaits.

Committing to a Lifetime of Continued Positivity

In our journey through life, we encounter a myriad of experiences – highs and lows, joys and sorrows, triumphs and trials. Amidst these ebbs and flows, one constant remains: our perspective. The lens through which we view our experiences determines not just our reactions to them, but also their impact on our psyche. By committing to a lifetime of continued positivity, we pledge to approach every situation, every challenge, and every moment with an optimistic mindset. This commitment isn't about ignoring life's complexities or masking genuine feelings. It's about choosing to see the silver lining, even in the most daunting of storms. It's about recognizing that setbacks are often setups for even more significant comebacks. By anchoring ourselves in a positive mindset, we cultivate resilience, foster growth, and enable ourselves to bounce back with even greater vigor. Every day offers a new opportunity to strengthen this commitment. Each morning we rise presents a fresh canvas, waiting to be painted with our hopes, aspirations, and positive intentions. We have the power to dictate the narrative of our lives, and with continued positivity, we ensure that our story is one of hope, perseverance, and unwavering faith in the beauty of tomorrow.

As you close this chapter and move forward, remember that your commitment to positivity is a gift – to yourself and to the world around you. It radiates, influencing not just your personal journey but also inspiring those you cross paths with. In a world often marred by cynicism and doubt, your beacon of positivity becomes a source of hope and a testament to the enduring spirit of optimism. So, as you step into the next phase of your life, hold onto this commitment with unwavering dedication. Embrace each day with enthusiasm, cherish every experience as a learning opportunity, and always remember: the brightest days often follow the darkest nights. With continued positivity, every sunrise becomes a promise of better tomorrows, and every sunset, a reflection of a day well-lived. Commit to this beautiful journey, for in positivity, we find the true essence of life's art.

Appendix

Glossary

Affection: A gentle feeling of fondness.

Affirmation: A positive statement to challenge and control negative thoughts.

Anxiety: A feeling of unease, like fear or worry that can be mild or severe.

Awareness: Conscious recognition of facts, emotions, or sensations.

Boundaries: Limits defining acceptable behavior.

Chaos: Extreme confusion or disorder.

Cognition: Mental processes involved in gaining knowledge.

Cognitive Bias: A systematic pattern of deviation from norm in judgment.

Compassion: Sympathetic concern for the sufferings of others.

Conflict Resolution: Solving a disagreement or dispute.

Digital Consumption: Intake of content through digital devices.

Distorted Thoughts: Irrational beliefs reinforcing negative thinking.

Distraction: A thing preventing concentration.

Ego: A person's sense of self-worth.

Emotional Intelligence: Recognizing, understanding, and managing emotions.

Empathy: The ability to understand and share the feelings of another.

Feedback: Information about reactions to a product or action.

Gratitude: Feeling thankful or appreciative.

Guilty Pleasure: Enjoyment from activities that one sees as a minor vice.

Harmony: Agreement or consistency in actions or situations.

Inspiration: The process of being mentally stimulated.

Journaling: The act of writing down thoughts and feelings.

Limiting Belief: A belief that limits potential.

Listening: Actively paying attention to spoken words.

Mantra: A word or phrase repeated to aid meditation.

Meditation: A practice to focus the mind and achieve clarity.

Mindfulness: Being present and engaged in the moment.

Mindset: Beliefs shaping one's view of the world.

Motivation: A reason or reasons to act in a particular way.

Narrative: A story or account of events.

Negativity: Pessimistic attitudes or views.

Obstacle: A thing that blocks progress.

Optimism: Hopefulness and confidence about future outcomes.

Perspective: A particular attitude or view towards something.

Positivity: A tendency to be optimistic.

Reflection: Serious thought or contemplation.

Relationship Dynamics: Patterns of interaction in relationships.

Resilience: The ability to bounce back from adversity.

Romantic Relationship: A bond based on love and trust.

Self-awareness: Consciousness of one's own character and feelings.

Self-compassion: Kindness towards oneself.

Sensory Experience: Perception by the senses.

Social Media: Digital platforms for content sharing and interaction.

Stress: Physical or emotional tension from challenges.

Validation: Recognition or affirmation of validity.

Vulnerability: Exposure to harm or criticism.

Wellness: The state of good health.

Workplace Relationships: Interactions with individuals at work.

Recommended Reading

"The Happiness Advantage: The Seven Principles of Positive Psychology That Fuel Success and Performance at Work" by Shawn Achor

Achor delves into the world of positive psychology and how happiness can be a significant advantage in our personal and professional lives. His insights are backed by extensive research and provide practical advice.

"The Untethered Soul: The Journey Beyond Yourself" by Michael A. Singer

This book provides a transformative exploration of consciousness, self-awareness, and spirituality. Singer presents a framework for letting go of limiting beliefs and stepping into a life of freedom and happiness.

"Drive: The Surprising Truth About What Motivates Us" by Daniel H. Pink

Pink explores the intricacies of human motivation, arguing that autonomy, mastery, and purpose drive us more than external rewards or punishments. This book is an eye-opener for understanding what truly motivates us in the realms of work, relationships, and personal growth.

"The Power of Now: A Guide to Spiritual Enlightenment" by Eckhart Tolle

Tolle's classic work emphasizes the importance of living in the present moment and letting go of past regrets and future anxieties. It offers a profound exploration of mindfulness and how being present can transform our lives.

"Grit: The Power of Passion and Perseverance" by Angela Duckworth

Duckworth presents compelling evidence that passion and perseverance (or "grit") play a more significant role in success than raw talent. This book provides insights into how cultivating grit can lead to greater achievements and satisfaction in life.

Bibliography

Chapter 1. Benefits of Positive Thinking

Seligman, M. E. P. (2002). Authentic happiness: Using the new positive psychology to realize your potential for lasting fulfillment. New York: Free Press.

Fredrickson, B. L. (2009). Positivity: Groundbreaking research reveals how to embrace the hidden strength of positive emotions, overcome negativity, and thrive. Crown Archetype.

Diener, E., & Seligman, M. E. (2002). Very happy people. Psychological Science, 13(1), 81-84.

Dweck, C. S. (2006). Mindset: The new psychology of success. New York: Random House.

Emmons, R. A. (2007). Thanks!: How the new science of gratitude can make you happier. Houghton Mifflin Harcourt.

Bandura, A. (1982). Self-efficacy mechanism in human agency. American Psychologist, 37(2), 122.

Snyder, C. R. et al. (1991). The will and the ways: development and validation of an individual-differences measure of hope. Journal of Personality and Social Psychology, 60(4), 570.

Chapter 2. Learning about Mindfulness

Kabat-Zinn, J. (1990). Full catastrophe living: Using the wisdom of your body and mind to face stress, pain, and illness. New York: Delacorte Press.

Brown, K. W., & Ryan, R. M. (2003). The benefits of being present: Mindfulness and its role in psychological well-being. Journal of Personality and Social Psychology, 84(4), 822.

Williams, M., & Penman, D. (2011). Mindfulness: An eight-week plan for finding peace in a frantic world. Rodale.

Baer, R. A. (2003). Mindfulness training as a clinical intervention: A conceptual and empirical review. Clinical Psychology: Science and Practice, 10(2), 125-143.

Turkle, S. (2011). Alone together: Why we expect more from technology and less from each other. Basic Books.

Lipton, B. H. (2005). The biology of belief: Unleashing the power of consciousness, matter & miracles. Santa Rosa, CA: Mountain of Love/Elite Books.

Emmons, R. A., & McCullough, M. E. (2003). Counting blessings versus burdens: An experimental investigation of gratitude and subjective well-being in daily life. Journal of Personality and Social Psychology, 84(2), 377.

Chapter 3. Understanding and Developing Emotional Intelligence

Goleman, D. (1995). Emotional intelligence. New York: Bantam Books.

Salovey, P., & Mayer, J. D. (1990). Emotional intelligence. Imagination, cognition and personality, 9(3), 185-211.

Eysenck, M. W., & Calvo, M. G. (1992). Anxiety and performance: The processing efficiency theory. Cognition & Emotion, 6(6), 409-434.

Brown, B. (2012). Daring greatly: How the courage to be vulnerable transforms the way we live, love, parent, and lead. Gotham.

Wegner, D. M. (1994). Ironic processes of mental control. Psychological Review, 101(1), 34.

Newport, C. (2016). Deep work: Rules for focused success in a distracted world. Grand Central Publishing.

Gottman, J. M., & Silver, N. (1999). The seven principles for making marriage work. New York: Crown Publishers.

Chapter 4. Understanding Your Own Mindset

Dweck, C. S. (2006). Mindset: The new psychology of success. New York: Random House.

Eysenck, M. W., & Calvo, M. G. (1992). Anxiety and performance: The processing efficiency theory. Cognition & Emotion, 6(6), 409-434.

Wegner, D. M. (1994). Ironic processes of mental control. Psychological Review, 101(1), 34.

Bandura, A. (1982). Self-efficacy mechanism in human agency. American Psychologist, 37(2), 122.

Ekman, P., Davidson, R. J., & Friesen, W. V. (1990). The Duchenne smile: Emotional expression and brain physiology: II. Journal of Personality and Social Psychology, 58(2), 342.

Strack, F., Martin, L. L., & Stepper, S. (1988). Inhibiting and facilitating conditions of the human smile: A nonobtrusive test of the facial feedback hypothesis. Journal of Personality and Social Psychology, 54(5), 768.

Fredrickson, B. L. (2001). The role of positive emotions in positive psychology. American Psychologist, 56(3), 218-226.

Chapter 5. Easy Actions to Increase Positive Thinking

Byrne, R. (2006). The Secret. Atria Books/Beyond Words.

Chodron, P. (1994). Start where you are: A guide to compassionate living. Shambhala Publications.

Kabat-Zinn, J. (1994). Wherever you go, there you are: Mindfulness meditation in everyday life. Hyperion.

Benson, H. (1975). The relaxation response. New York: Morrow.

Schwartz, J. M. (2002). The mind & the brain: Neuroplasticity and the power of mental force. Harper Perennial.

Clear, J. (2018). Atomic habits: An easy & proven way to build good habits & break bad ones. Random House.

Emmons, R. A., & McCullough, M. E. (2003). Counting blessings versus burdens: An experimental investigation of gratitude and subjective well-being in daily life. Journal of Personality and Social Psychology, 84(2), 377.

Chapter 6. Spreading the Positivity

Fredrickson, B. L. (2001). The role of positive emotions in positive psychology: The broaden-and-build theory of positive emotions. American Psychologist, 56(3), 218.

Grant, A. (2013). Give and take: A revolutionary approach to success. Viking.

Csikszentmihalyi, M. (1990). Flow: The psychology of optimal experience. Harper & Row.

Tugade, M. M., & Fredrickson, B. L. (2007). Regulation of positive emotions: Emotion regulation strategies that promote resilience. Journal of Happiness Studies, 8(3), 311-333.

Lyubomirsky, S. (2008). The how of happiness: A scientific approach to getting the life you want. Penguin Press.

Otake, K., Shimai, S., Tanaka-Matsumi, J., Otsui, K., & Fredrickson, B. L. (2006). Happy people become happier through kindness: A counting kindnesses intervention. Journal of Happiness Studies, 7(3), 361-375.

Fowler, J. H., & Christakis, N. A. (2008). Dynamic spread of happiness in a large social network: Longitudinal analysis over 20 years in the Framingham Heart Study. BMJ, 337, a2338.

Chapter 7. Practicing Gratitude to Improve Positive Thinking

Emmons, R. A., & McCullough, M. E. (2003). Counting blessings versus burdens: An experimental investigation of gratitude and subjective well-being in daily life. Journal of Personality and Social Psychology, 84(2), 377.

Lyubomirsky, S., Sheldon, K. M., & Schkade, D. (2005). Pursuing happiness: The architecture of sustainable change. Review of General Psychology, 9(2), 111.

Wood, A. M., Froh, J. J., & Geraghty, A. W. (2010). Gratitude and well-being: A review and theoretical integration. Clinical Psychology Review, 30(7), 890-905.

Brown, B. (2010). The gifts of imperfection: Let go of who you think you're supposed to be and embrace who you are. Hazelden Publishing.

Csikszentmihalyi, M., & Robinson, R. E. (1990). The art of seeing: An interpretation of the aesthetic encounter. Getty Publications.

Watkins, P. C., Woodward, K., Stone, T., & Kolts, R. L. (2003). Gratitude and happiness: Development of a measure of gratitude and relationships with subjective well-being. Social Behavior and Personality: An International Journal, 31(5), 431-451.

Algoe, S. B. (2012). Find, remind, and bind: The functions of gratitude in everyday relationships. Social and Personality Psychology Compass, 6(6), 455-469.

Chapter 8. Becoming More Aware of Negative Thinking

Beck, A. T. (1976). Cognitive therapy and the emotional disorders. New York: International Universities Press.

Hayes, S. C., Strosahl, K., & Wilson, K. G. (1999). Acceptance and commitment therapy: An experiential approach to behavior change. Guilford Press.

Burns, D. D. (1980). Feeling good: The new mood therapy. New York: William Morrow and Company.

Ellis, A. (1962). Reason and emotion in psychotherapy. Secaucus, NJ: The Citadel Press.

Neff, K. D. (2003). The development and validation of a scale to measure self-compassion. Self and Identity, 2(3), 223-250.

Fredrickson, B. L., & Joiner, T. (2002). Positive emotions trigger upward spirals toward emotional well-being. Psychological Science, 13(2), 172-175.

Tugade, M. M., & Fredrickson, B. L. (2004). Resilient individuals use positive emotions to bounce back from negative emotional experiences. Journal of Personality and Social Psychology, 86(2), 320.

Chapter 9. The Role of Relationships in Positive Thinking

Gable, S. L., & Reis, H. T. (2010). Good news! Capitalizing on positive events in an interpersonal context. Advances in Experimental Social Psychology, 42, 195-257.

Gottman, J. M. (1994). What predicts divorce? The relationship between marital processes and marital outcomes. Hillsdale, NJ: Lawrence Erlbaum.

Fehr, B. (2008). Friendship processes. Sage Publications.

Berscheid, E., & Reis, H. T. (1998). Attraction and close relationships. In D. T. Gilbert, S. T. Fiske, & G. Lindzey (Eds.), The handbook of social psychology, Vol. 2 (4th ed., pp. 193-281). Boston: McGraw-Hill.

Amabile, T. M., & Kramer, S. J. (2011). The progress principle: Using small wins to ignite joy, engagement, and creativity at work. Harvard Business Review Press.

DePaulo, B. M., & Morris, W. L. (2006). The unrecognized stereotyping and discrimination against singles.

Current Directions in Psychological Science, 15(5), 251-254.

Feeney, B. C., & Collins, N. L. (2015). A new look at social support: A theoretical perspective on thriving through relationships. Personality and Social Psychology Review, 19(2), 113-147.

Chapter 10. Maintaining Positive Thinking in Chaos and Rougher Times

Seligman, M. E. P. (2011). Flourish: A visionary new understanding of happiness and well-being. Free Press.

Bonanno, G. A. (2004). Loss, trauma, and human resilience: Have we underestimated the human capacity to thrive after extremely aversive events? American Psychologist, 59(1), 20.

Carver, C. S. (1998). Resilience and thriving: Issues, models, and linkages. Journal of Social Issues, 54(2), 245-266.

Masten, A. S. (2001). Ordinary magic: Resilience processes in development. American Psychologist, 56(3), 227.

Lyubomirsky, S. (2013). The myths of happiness: What should make you happy, but doesn't, what shouldn't make you happy, but does. Penguin.

Diener, E., & Biswas-Diener, R. (2008). Happiness: Unlocking the mysteries of psychological wealth. Blackwell Publishing.

Tugade, M. M., & Fredrickson, B. L. (2007). Regulation of positive emotions: Emotion regulation strategies that promote resilience. Journal of Happiness Studies, 8(3), 311-333.

Chapter 11. Tips and Tricks to Keep You Going

Louv, R. (2005). Last child in the woods: Saving our children from nature-deficit disorder. Algonquin Books.

Csikszentmihalyi, M. (1997). Finding flow: The psychology of engagement with everyday life. Basic Books.

Levitin, D. J. (2006). This is your brain on music: The science of a human obsession. Dutton.

Twenge, J. M., & Campbell, W. K. (2018). The narcissism epidemic: Living in the age of entitlement. Free Press.

Newport, C. (2016). Deep work: Rules for focused success in a distracted world. Grand Central Publishing.

Greenfield, S. (2015). Mind change: How digital technologies are leaving their mark on our brains. Random House.

Fredrickson, B. L. (2009). Positivity: Top-notch research reveals the 3-to-1 ratio that will change your life. Crown.

Further sources:

Optimism and Pessimism, Max Roser and Mohamed Nagdy (2014) - "Optimism and Pessimism". Published online at OurWorldInData.org. Retrieved from: 'https://ourworldindata.org/optimism-pessimism'

The Power of Positive Thinking, John Hopkins Medicine, September 3, 2022, The Johns Hopkins University, The Johns Hopkins Hospital, https://www.hopkinsmedicine.org/health/wellness-and-prevention/the-power-of-positive-thinking

https://www.mindful.org/what-is-mindfulness/ , Mindful Staff, July 8, 2020, Well-Being, https://www.mindful.org/what-is-mindfulness/

How the Benefits of Positive Thinking Will Help Your Mind and Body, Seraine Page, November 8, 2021, Total Wellness, https://info.totalwellnesshealth.com/blog/benefits-of-positive-thinking

Disclaimer

The information provided in the book "The Art of Positive Thinking: Emotional Intelligence I Affirmation I Eliminate Negative Thinking" is intended for general informational and educational purposes only. The author and publisher of this book are not licensed therapists, psychologists, or medical professionals, and the content within should not be considered a substitute for professional advice, diagnosis, or treatment.

Readers are encouraged to seek the guidance of qualified professionals, such as mental health practitioners or medical experts, for any personal or emotional issues they may be experiencing. The strategies, techniques, and exercises presented in this book are based on the author's research and personal experiences, but individual results may vary.

The author and publisher make no representations or warranties regarding the accuracy, completeness, or suitability of the information contained in this book. Furthermore, the author and publisher disclaim any responsibility for any actions taken or not taken by readers as a result of reading this book. The choice to implement any suggestions or recommendations from this book is entirely at the reader's discretion and risk.

Reading and utilizing the content of this book does not guarantee specific outcomes, and the author and publisher shall not be held liable for any direct or indirect consequences, including but not limited to, personal injury, loss, or damage arising from the use of the information provided herein.

By reading this book, readers acknowledge that they have read and understood this disclaimer, and they agree to use the information within responsibly and in conjunction with professional guidance where necessary.

Made in the USA
Las Vegas, NV
21 November 2023

81170917R00104